DEBRETT'S
QUEEN VICTORIA'S
JUBILEES
1887 & 1897

Compiled by

CAROLINE CHAPMAN &
PAUL RABEN

Foreword H. B. Brooks-Baker

DEBRETT'S PEERAGE LIMITED

Photographic Acknowledgements

We would like to thank the following Picture Libraries for providing many of the illustrations: the Cooper Bridgeman Library, the Guildhall Art Gallery, the Mansell Collection, Popperfoto and the Archives of Weidenfeld & Nicolson Ltd.

We are also grateful to the British Library and the British Newspaper Library at Colindale for their kind permission to reproduce illustrations from various magazines of the period.

Our thanks are also due to the following photographers: Ray Gardner, Geoff Goode Photographics, Angelo Hornak and Eileen Tweedy.

© Debrett's Peerage Ltd 1977
Published by Debrett's Peerage Ltd
23 Mossop Street, London sw3

ISBN 0 905649 04 4

Distributed by Seeley, Service & Cooper Ltd
196 Shaftesbury Avenue, London, wc2h 8jl

Designed by Humphrey Stone at the Compton Press Ltd.,
The Old Brewery, Tisbury, Salisbury, Wilts.
Text printed at Unwin Bros. Ltd., The Gresham Press,
Old Woking, Surrey.
Colour at P.R.T. Offset Ltd., 2 Brandon Road, London n7.
and bound at Webb Son & Co. Ltd., 24-28 Friern Park,
London n12.

P.TO.

HT SOAP

NEW ZEALAND

NEW SOUTH WALES

VICTORIA

1887

PPOINTMENT TO HER MAJESTY.

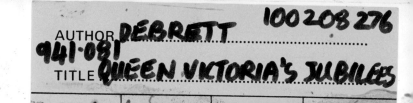

DEBRET
QUEEN VIC
JUBIL
1887 & 1

frontispiece Queen Victoria aged forty-seven, 1866

FOREWORD

The following pages illustrate the sentiment of the British people during the two great festivities of Queen Victoria's reign. The Golden Jubilee and the Diamond Jubilee. The articles and illustrations were chosen from leading magazines of the time so that the reader can appreciate the atmosphere of that period. Also included are protographs by eminent photographers.

In many ways it is more interesting to see an advertisement of the time than a picture of the 50,000 troops which marched in the Queen's second Jubilee. The romantic emissaries who appeared in London from almost every country in the world were seen by thousands of people, but the printed ephemera of the time was seen and read by millions.

The Golden Jubilee of 1887 should have been the second of Queen Victoria's great festivals, but alas her husband, Prince Albert, died the year before the Silver Jubilee was scheduled, and naturally celebrations and festivities could not take place.

The celebrations of 1887 began under a large cloud, which did not disappear until the Queen herself realised that a Golden Jubilee meant everything to her people, who were determined to see their Queen cheerful again. In June she had said 'The day has come and I am alone', but to think of herself as alone, when hundreds of cousins, aunts and uncles arrived from every great European House to pay homage to the leader of their family, seems strange to us today. The Battenbergs, Bernadottes, Bourbons, Bourbon-Parmas, Braganças, Coburgs, Glücksburgs, Hapsburgs, Hesses, Hohenzollerns, Mecklenburg-Strelitzs, Mecklenburg-Schwerins, Romanoffs, Savoys, Wittelsbachs, and all the other great names of Europe were there *en masse*. Queen Victoria spent three days in London from June 20th until June 23rd. No human being could have been busier, or more fully occupied than she, and many who saw her that summer, thought that she looked far younger than her 68 years, despite having to be host to her countless relations. The great family dinner of June 20th found the Queen between the King of Denmark and the King of Greece. When she met the diplomatic corps in the great ballroom, her conversation on international subjects was as scintillating and precise as her dissertations on family problems. The greatest of all the celebrations, however, was the thanksgiving service in Westminster Abbey, which took place on the bright cloudless day of June 21st.

The procession consisted first of her closest relations followed by her many direct descendants. The colours of the uniforms of everyone, from the Prince of Wales, who was dressed in the bright red of a British Field Marshal, to Prince Albert Victor, in a uniform of the Hussars, were dazzling. Some felt that the Crown Prince of Germany (Fritz, the Queen's son-in-law) stole the show, with his white uniform and eagle crowned helmet giving a comic opera effect to the whole affair, but perhaps the group that really captured people's imagination was the Indian cavalry.

The Queen did not wear colourful clothes for the occasion, but deigned only to replace her black bonnet for a white one, which sported white feathers with yards of white Alençon lace. She, who never ceased to think of herself as a solitary person surounded by strangers said: 'I sat alone, Oh! without my beloved husband, for whom this would have been such a proud day!'

In every way the Golden Jubilee emphasised to all that the Queen was head, not only of the largest royal family in the world, but also the most important, and not a person would have believed that ten years later an even greater Jubilee would take place. The Coburgs, the family that Prince Bismarck bellicosely referred to as the 'Stud farm of Europe', at last had their finest hour. The heyday for the great protestant Royals had arrived, and England as the most powerful protestant country of the world, was convinced that the sun would never set on her Empire. This was the last great flowering of European monarchy.

Queen Victoria would certainly not have been considered an unusual or greatly talented person in a different setting. She was the possessor of considerable gifts, but no one would deny that she was born in the right place at the right time, and had made the most of her God-given abilities.

The Diamond Jubilee of 1897 captured the imagination of the Queen's loyal subjects in every corner of the Empire. She and her people would have been amazed had they realized that Imperialism was to last such a very short time longer.

The year of 1897 brought an unusually hot and bright summer for the celebrations which lasted week after week. The banner in St James's stated proudly 'Queen of earthly Queens'. Till then there had never been a monarch who filled this role, and there never would be again.

The three hundred thousand pounds spent on decorations in London was proof to all that England was in an extravagant mood.

The Times wrote: 'There are two factors in the celebrations which transcend all others in their significance as symbols of the Imperial unity. One is the revered personality of the Queen, the other is the superb condition of Her Majesty's fleet'. The Royal Navy had certainly become the second most important symbol of the Empire; the Queen naturally was the first. Almost two hundred ships were dressed at Spithead for the Royal review that year.

Few people who took part on these two great occasions were able to remember Queen Victoria when she came to the throne in 1837, and one must be aware that much of the Empire, eighteen territories in all, had been acquired after she ascended the throne. Queen Victoria was very proud of the fact that a quarter of the people in the world, and almost a quarter of the land, were under her rule. Whether she realised that the celebrations in 1897 were in reality a demonstration of British might is unknown. English upper middle class was emulated everywhere throughout the world, in dress, in speech, in sport, and strange as it may seem, in some of their eating habits.

Queen Victoria was Supreme Governor of the Church of England, and Defender of the Faith. She hoped that her subjects overseas would accept her religion, and was immensely interested in the fate of the missionaries sent out from England. It was overlooked by the English at the time that not everyone was ready to become an Anglican, or even be prepared to accept the fact that the world was made primarily for the white man.

The Queen, with the help of Disraeli, had convinced herself that the Empire was indestructible. She had been urged by him to accept the title Empress of India, and it was he who helped to convince her that she was undisputed Empress of the world. She was in many ways a very practical person who read every word of every document, and was most conscious about her duties, but the influence that some and particularly Disraeli with his saturnine looks had over her was enormous. Her husband, Albert of Saxe-Coburg and Gotha, had wielded an overwhelming power like that of her Uncle King Leopold I of the Belgians, and Napoleon III of France. The way her mind could be ruled by her heart is best illustrated by her support and love of Louis Napoleon. For years she had been devoted to, and sympathised with, King Louis Philippe of France, but it was the personality of the great Napoleon's nephew, which brought her into the Bonaparte camp. The Queen's loyalty to those who influenced her was unquestionable. The forty years that Eugenie, Empress of France and wife of Louis Philippe, spent in England (most of it as a guest of Queen Victoria), was proof of the English monarch's unyielding devotion to those who had her ear and support.

Queen Victoria's subjects were also immensely loyal to her, not only because of their love and admiration for the monarch, but because the mystique of the crown had mesmerised them. When she returned to the Palace after her last Jubilee, she was choked with emotion by the demonstrations of loyalty manifested by her loving subjects. The success of the Queen's Diamond Jubilee would be remembered for ever. The Queen recognised that the republicanism which was rampant before 1887 had vanished for ever.

H. B. BROOKS-BAKER
Paris mcmlxxvi

THE QUEEN'S WIDOWHOOD.

It was naturally some time ere her Majesty, who had the fullest sympathy of the people in her bereavement, felt able to resume the public part of the onerous and heavy duties of the Sovereign. In the uninterrupted discharge, however, of the responsible and delicate daily tasks which fall to the lot of the occupant of the Throne, always performed with zealous regularity by her Majesty, the Queen insensibly found a mitigation of her great grief. Work is the great solacer. And the marriages of one after another of her sons and daughters, and the increasing cares of her ever-growing Empire, gradually weaned her mind from her crushing sorrow. In the first year of widowhood, on the First of July, her Majesty assisted at the quiet wedding of Princess Alice and Prince Louis of Hesse, at Osborne; and later, in 1862, the Queen paid another visit to Germany. Though her Majesty had not the nerve to take a conspicuous part in the marriage ceremony of her eldest son on the Tenth of March, 1863, the Queen witnessed the union of the Prince of Wales and the charming Princess Alexandra of Denmark from the private Royal balcony in St. George's Chapel, Windsor. Not until 1866 did her Majesty feel strong enough to emerge from her semi-retirement, and to open Parliament in person—a dignified and regal ceremonial, which the Queen last performed, as delineated by our Artist, in 1886. In the year 1867 appeared the first of those naturally-written Royal publications, which, it is no exaggeration to say, have had the effect of drawing yet closer the bonds of affection which unite her loyal subjects to the frank and gracious Lady who so openly laid bare her heart, and let all the world know the every-day doings of the most exalted but still purest of households. "The Early Years of H.R.H. the Prince Consort," edited under the instructions of the Queen herself by Lieut.-Gen. the Hon. C. Grey, occasioned widespread interest; and was quickly followed by her Majesty's own diary, "Leaves from the Journal of our Life in the Highlands, from 1841 to 1861," which exquisitely simple and open narration of Court life, and of our Queen's thoughts and opinions on passing events, has since been continued, to the delight of the reading public.

Her Majesty has been very fortunate in these latter days to have so willing, affable, and indefatigable a deputy at hand as the Prince of Wales, the most popular man in England, and, indeed, the most popular Prince in Christendom—his popularity being enhanced by the sweet charm of his generally beloved wife, H.R.H. the Princess of Wales. Every city in the land is familiar with the genial visage of our blonde, blue-eyed Prince and with the fascinating face of our smiling Princess. For countless public and charitable institutions have been inaugurated by their Royal Highnesses with a captivating bonhomie all their own in every part of the Kingdom. The warm regard in which the Prince is held by reason of this zealous and cheerful performance of ceremonial duties was notably shown when he was stricken with fever, and lay almost next door to death in the winter of 1871-72 at Sandringham, where the anxious Mother, and loving sister-nurse from Hesse-Darmstadt, visited him—the whole nation suspensefully scanning each bulletin published. When, brought back to life, the Prince proceeded with the Queen and Princess to St. Paul's on the national Thanksgiving Day (February the Twenty-seventh, 1872), the enthusiasm of the populace knew no bounds.

We pass by the Royal marriages at which her Majesty figured, as each is recorded near our Illustrations of the most recent of these ceremonies. To indicate the multifarious nature of the duties the Queen has been called upon to perform during the past fifteen years, let us briefly mention her Majesty's drive to Victoria Park amid the cheers of East-Enders in the April of 1873; the Queen's escorting of the Duke of Edinburgh's bonnie bride to Buckingham Palace on the snowy Twenty-third of January, 1874; the decoration of Garnet Wolseley's Ashantee heroes at Gosport in the following April; the opening of a new wing of the London Hospital in 1876, when her Majesty also paid another visit to Germany; her journey in 1877 to Hughenden, to see Lord Beaconsfield, the then Premier, who had on May Day of the previous year caused the Queen to be proclaimed Empress of India (and the death of which able statesman and accomplished novelist on April 19, 1881, occasioned general grief); her Majesty's trip on May 6, 1882, to Epping Forest to declare it open to the public for ever; the review of Tel-el-Kebir troops in St. James's Park on the succeeding Eighteenth of November; and the opening of the Royal Courts of Justice in the Strand on Dec. 4 following. The dark shadow that falls on the palace and cottage alike caused renewed mourning in the Royal family when Princess Alice expired in 1878; and again when the Queen's youngest son, the Duke of Albany, died in the flower of his manhood at Cannes in 1884.

left A retrospective article from the *Penny Illustrated Paper* deftly glosses over the infrequency of the Queen's public appearances since Prince Albert's death in 1861. In our own age, when the Monarchy is virtually public property, it is less easy to understand how her initial shock was allowed to congeal into morbid hibernation. Her reliance on the Prince's guidance had been absolute and when he died, there were no substitute strengths at hand. She had, in youth, been a high spirited and restless girl but now a physical lassitude seized her; the sole object of her interest was the design of the great Mausoleum at Frogmore – 'for us' – and a host of memorials great and small to the memory of 'the dear, dear, protecting hand'.

opposite above left The Queen and the Prince Consort at Osborne House in 1859.

opposite above right The Queen with Princess Helena (*left*) and Princess Louise of Hesse (Princess Alice) in front of a painting of the Prince Consort at Balmoral.

opposite below The Blue Room at Windsor where Prince Albert died from typhoid at 10.45 p.m. on December 14th, 1861; in this room both George IV and William IV had died. There were two beds in the room so that the delirious Prince could be moved from one to the other to make him more comfortable. It is thought that he died in the bed nearest the camera. The Queen held his hand at the end, with three of the royal children, the Prince of Wales and the Princesses Alice and Helena, together with a dozen or so courtiers looking on.

The Queen visited the deathbed many times before the body was removed, though she gave orders that the sheets were not to be changed. The room was later 'beautifully though simply' decorated and fresh china and pictures were added as well as the bust of the Prince seen on a plinth between the beds on which were laid evergreen sprays. His hat, gloves and cane were placed on the dressing table and each day until the Queen's death forty years later, hot water and clean towels were brought in every evening. The Queen described the significance of the petrified deathchamber: 'When in an agony of loneliness, grief and despair, I kneel by that bed where He left us, decked with flowers and pray *earnestly* to be enabled to be courageous, patient and calm, and to be guided by my darling to *do what He* would wish; then a calm seems to come over me, a certainty my anguish is seen and heard *not* in vain, and I feel *lifted above* this miserable earth of sorrows.

THE QUEEN'S JUBILEE

The summer of 1887 was one of exceptional fineness, but there was no day more brilliant than Tuesday, June 21, when the Queen returned thanks at Westminster Abbey for the fifty years of her reign. Among the vast crowd of dignitaries, and the foreign representatives, the wearing of uniforms was the order of the day, so that the whole ceremony blazed with colour. Many schemes and funds were set on foot to commemorate a year of pageantry, none more fittingly than that of founding the Imperial Institute at South Kensington.

JUNE 20, 1887

To-day the QUEEN completes the fiftieth year of a reign prosperous and glorious beyond any recorded in the annals of England. To few Sovereigns has it been granted to celebrate the Jubilee of their accession, and among these few we know of no Queen or Empress. In the early morning on the 20th of June, 1837, the ARCHBISHOP of CANTERBURY and the LORD CHAMBERLAIN hastened to Kensington Palace to rouse the young PRINCESS VICTORIA from her sleep and to announce to her that by her uncle's death she had succeeded to the Throne. From that moment onwards the QUEEN has been deeply impressed with the responsibilities of power, and has held her sovereignty to be a sacred trust for the benefit of the peoples under her rule. No constitutional Monarch has shown a more consistent respect for popular liberties or a clearer conception of royal duties. The QUEEN has this week the reward she must prize beyond all else, the spontaneous expression of national enthusiasm. The spectacle, which will culminate in the splendour of to-morrow's Thanksgiving Service in Westminster Abbey, in the Royal Procession through the streets, and in the illuminations of the evening, may well fix the attention, not only of all sorts and conditions of Englishmen, Scotchmen, and Irishmen, but of exalted and eminent personages from all civilized States. The Sovereigns of Europe will be fully represented in the historic scene, and seldom, perhaps, have so many princely visitors assembled to take part in such a ceremony. The HEIR APPARENT to the Imperial Throne of Germany will be present, with his eldest son; the CROWN PRINCE, the successor to the Austro-Hungarian Monarchy, will be there, with the KING of the BELGIANS, the KING of DENMARK, the KING of GREECE, the KING of SAXONY, the CROWN PRINCE of SWEDEN, the GRAND-DUKE SERGE of RUSSIA, PRINCE LUDWIG of BAVARIA, the CROWN PRINCE of PORTUGAL, the DUKE of AOSTA (formerly King of Spain), and many others, including representative princes of our Indian Empire, with MAHARAJAH HOLKAR at their head. But the most impressive element in the scene will be the demeanour of the people. Britons, in spite of a confirmed habit of grumbling, look upon their ancient institutions with steadfast affection and reverence, and their attachment to the monarchy has been blended with respect for the character of the QUEEN. Nothing in the rich and various history of the past fifty years is more worthy of record than the purification and refinement of social life and manners to which the influence of the Court has most powerfully contributed. Those who are familiar with the current literature of the early part of the century will most readily acknowledge how vast a change has taken place in the tone in which royalty and royal persons are spoken of. That change is mainly due to the conduct of the QUEEN, in public and in private, since her accession, and to the wisdom of the counsels by which she was long guided. It must ever be remembered that for this and other faithful services the nation owes a deep debt of gratitude to the memory of the PRINCE CONSORT.

If we look back over the half-century which has elapsed since the 20th of June, 1837, we see how stormy were the political waters on which the young SOVEREIGN embarked, and how much she needed the aid of a loyal and devoted adviser....

above left and right Extracts from *The Times* leader June 20th, 1887. At this stage the word Jubilee connoted fifty years; the concept of a Silver Jubilee was not introduced until 1935 for George v, who was then 70, and unwell. It is extraordinarily similar in tone to the recent *Times* leader on the present Queen and neither can be put down to mere journalistic unction; the sense of duty and wholesome family life, which marked both reigns were then, as now, highly valued. Royalties from 14 monarchies visited London for the Jubilee; only four of these have survived.

left Princess Victoria receiving news of her accession in the early morning of June 20th, 1837. King William had died shortly after 2 a.m. at Windsor and Archbishop Howley and the Lord Chamberlain, Lord Conynghame travelled directly to Kensington Palace arriving at about 5 a.m.

The Princess' mother, the Duchess of Kent would not at first allow them to see the still sleeping Princess; Lord Conynghame then demanded to see 'the Queen' and at about 6 a.m. she was awakened and came downstairs to her sitting-room which she entered 'alone'. On being told of the death of her 'poor good uncle' she swiftly extended her hand for her visitors to kiss. She wrote in her diary: 'I am young and perhaps in many ways, though not in all things, inexperienced, but I am sure that very few have more real good will and more real desire to do what is fit and right than I have'.

opposite right In 1887 the technique of photographic reproduction was still in its infancy and engravings were cut by hand after the original photographs.

1837 HANDSOMELY ILLUSTRATED

KENSINGTON PALACE
HER MAJESTY'S BIRTHPLACE

JUBILEE LIFE OF QUEEN VICTORIA

THE QUEEN ON THE MORNING OF HER ACCESSION

1887

WITH A BEAUTIFUL COLOURED PORTRAIT OF HER MAJESTY

above left Princess Victoria aged 4; painting by J. P. Denning 1823.

above right Princess Victoria aged 15 with her mother, the Duchess of Kent; from a drawing by Sir William Hayter in 1834. The Duchess was a Bavarian princess of the House of Leiningen, spoke little or no English and due to a combination of bad luck and a spendthrift husband, lived most of her life cheerfully on the brink of financial ruin. She was a good natured silly woman who made the upbringing of a possible Queen of England (Victoria at birth was only fifth in line of succession) her life's work. Possibly she overdid it for in later years Victoria reminisced that her childhood was 'sad and lonely'. 'I was extremely crushed and hardly dared say a word'.

right Princess Victoria after a bout of typhoid in 1835. Victoria never excelled at sketching portraits though she showed promise in some of her landscape sketches. What she prized above all was 'a likeness' and this priority dominated her artistic interest throughout her life. The invention of photography, now not so far off, was, to her, like a dispensation from on high.

STANDS ENGLAND WHERE SHE DID?

UNDER the pretext of rejoicing over Her Majesty's Jubilee, the people of England, or those who speak for them through Press, platform, and pulpit, have been indulging in a vast amount of self-glorification. The year 1837 has been compared with 1887 from many different points of view, greatly to the disadvantage of the state of things that existed at the earlier date. The general tone of such comparisons is in fact highly optimistic, but unfortunately optimism is often quite as ill-founded as pessimism. No one will deny that in many ways the world in general, and the British Empire in particular, has made progress of a kind since 1837; but it would be folly to say that England is in every respect in a better position now than she was fifty years ago. We have no particular desire to say unpleasant things, or to strike a discordant note in the midst of the general chorus of jubilation; but we try at all times to look fairly at facts, even though they are not very pleasant ones; and we have no special liking for a fool's paradise even in Jubilee time. On one point we feel certain that England has *not* advanced since 1837. Her position among the Powers of Europe is not what it was then. She has lost, not gained, in influence and importance in the councils of the world. Our last fifty years of foreign policy have not been a success. The sooner we recognise this the better. The first step towards putting our armaments into a satisfactory condition was taken when we realised that our soldiers and sailors were being provided by incompetent officials with bursting guns, jamming cartridges, and bending bayonets; and just in the same way the first step towards regaining our old position in the world will be taken when we clearly recognise that, through the unfaithfulness or the incompetency of those who have directed English foreign policy, and through the general ignorance and carelessness of the public at large, England does not stand where she did fifty years ago, but is rapidly becoming *une quantité négligeable* in international politics.

It would be easy to trace in detail the downward course by which England, despite her wealth, her world-wide Empire, and her claim to be the mistress of the seas, has all but lost her position as a Great Power. Here we can only point to some of the main factors in the change. But first let us note that in 1837 the laurels of Waterloo and Trafalgar were still fresh, and in men's minds England was the Power that had successfully grappled with Napoleon, organised great coalitions against him, swept every hostile flag from the sea, and finally played a foremost part in rearranging the map of Europe at Vienna. We have been living ever since on the reputation acquired in those days, and our capital has diminished considerably. Especially we have lost in the last fifty years—

(1) By consenting, at Paris in 1856, to surrender our ancient maritime rights, and adopt new rules of naval warfare, which took from us our chief weapon as a maritime Power. England is no longer in any true sense mistress of the seas. We have been foolish enough to allow our right arm to be tied up. We have made military and not naval power the measure of national strength, although it is utterly hopeless for us to attempt to rival as a military Power the great armed nations of the Continent. In the second half of the last fifty years the armies of the great military Powers have increased enormously, while we have, by our own act, surrendered our power to attack them effectively on that element on which we are strong and they are weak. We say nothing of the growth of foreign navies. The question of the number of our ironclads and torpedo boats is of little importance compared to the question of the right and power to make use of them. This Declaration of Paris of 1856 has taken from us. Our first step towards regaining our old position must be to abrogate it.

(2) Although in these fifty years we have waged only one European war (and that a war of collusion, when we were agreed with our enemy rather than our ally), we have waged a great number of wars in Africa and Asia; wars for the most part unjust, waged without due cause, and without Declaration of War. Some of them no one now defends; others are defended only by those who are ignorant or deniers of the facts. Some of these wars have already borne their full fruit of disgrace, disaster, and difficulty. Of others we have still to feel the Nemesis. But the chief evil is that the public conscience has become so dulled that such wars are only condemned when they lead directly to failure, and that both the great political Parties condemn, not injustice, but unsuccessful injustice. Look at our Affghan wars. The first dates from 1838; it was waged on false pretences, by a Minister who was convicted by the House of Commons of having garbled and falsified the papers that he laid before the nation, in order to win support for an attack upon a friendly Prince. Yet that Minister, the late Lord Palmerston, is still held up to admiration as an ideal Foreign Secretary. Look at the Chinese wars, on the injustice of which we have the solemn judgment of an English Court of Law and the vote of the House of Commons—a vote reversed only by an appeal to popular passions, and that on a false issue. Finally, look at our Egyptian wars, begun by the bombardment in time of peace of a city of one of our allies. Enterprises like these have not merely been national crimes, but they have already been the source of national weakness and disaster. Our own injustice has been made the occasion of outrage against our Empire and our allies, and our own deeds have prevented us from raising any effectual protest.

(3) Then, too, we have betrayed and abandoned friends to whom we were pledged by solemn Treaties, and who would have been a bulwark to our Empire; and we have done this in the interest of our avowed enemies. England has taken a leading part in the dismemberment of Turkey. England abandoned Circassia to its fate by permitting the open violation of Treaties of which she herself was the author, and thus gave to Russia the base of operations for her advance in Central Asia, whereof men now begin to realise the full danger to our Empire in the East.

(4) There has been no consistency in our foreign policy. It has been an alternation of inaction based on weak and ignorant denial of coming danger, and spasmodic and ill-directed action when the danger could no longer be denied. Look at the articles in the *Times* on Central Asia from 1864 to 1878, the elaborate proof that Russia could not cross the steppes and deserts of Turkestan, and then the arguments that, even if she did, she would never menace India seriously. Remember Lord Salisbury's famous appeal to the "large maps." Then there was the threadbare joke a little later about *Merv*ousness, and the cheap jibes at Russophobia. And yet all this did not prevent such exploits as our last invasion of Affghanistan on the pretext of resisting Russian influence at Cabul. England has never yet had a consistent policy for ten years at a time. No wonder she fails where those who have a settled policy succeed.

(5) Finally, weakness and failure have been disguised under well-turned phrases. The surrender at Berlin was atoned for by the talk about "Peace with Honour." The invasion of Egypt was a "restoration of order." No one is long deceived by such devices. But for awhile men, in the fear and dread of real straightforward action, accept such phrases as a consolation when England has taken her part in one of those field days of Russian diplomacy which are known as European Conferences, or has been dragged into an unjustifiable aggression upon some half-barbarous Power.

Are these things true, or are they not? We declare that they are not only true, but capable of solid and evident proof from sources that are open to all the world. Would it not be well, for the sake of the years that are to come, for the sake of our position among nations, to look into this question of the character of our last fifty years of foreign policy? It is no question of Party politics. It is because such things have been made questions of Party politics that Ministers of both Parties have been able to involve England in so much weakness, folly, and crime. Is it not time to put a stop to such things before it is too late? Can we not, even at the eleventh hour, strive to be just? Only thus shall we be strong.

THE JUDGES OF ENGLAND.

XXX.—SIR ARTHUR KEKEWICH.

THE junior Judge of the High Court is a lucky man. For however really deserving he may be, he was certainly not a very distinguished Counsel, outside his own family circle, when he was made a Judge last November. All judicial appointments nowadays provoke criticism on one side or another; but never since Mr. Gladstone sent Sir Robert Collier straight up to the Judicial Committee has any such appointment raised such a storm of adverse criticism as fell upon the new Judge's head at

Queen Victoria with Princess Henry of Battenberg (*standing*), Princess Louis of Battenberg and Princess Alice on her lap. Shy, stout and overprotected, Beatrice was the least brilliant of Victoria's daughters. She was allowed to marry only on the condition she remained in England after marriage. She died in 1944.

THE GOLDEN JUBILEE OF 1887

There exists an early cinematograph of the Diamond Jubilee Thanksgiving Service held on the steps of St. Pauls Cathedral in 1897; a pioneer effort allowing us a hazy glimpse of the moving image of an old woman born in the reign of her grandfather King George III who had owned America. The two Jubilees of 1887 and 1897 were the grand finales of a century and a reign in which Englands power and influence reached the highest point of an upward curve that had started with the Tudors; in the next half-century much of it would have vanished.

The Golden Jubilee of 1887 was a less bombastic affair than the grand display of ten years later. Punch's Jubilee Ode entitled 'A peaceful Triumph' praised 'the lack of martial pomp that tyrants love':

Not with the ruthless Roman's proud parade
Of flaunting ensigns and of fettered foes,
Nor radiantly arrayed,
In pomp of purple such as fitly flows
From the stern Conqueror's shoulders, comes our Queen . . .

The Queen had scarcely been seen by her subjects, in 'pomp of purple' or otherwise, for 25 years and throughout the seventies, this invisibility, which cost the nation an annual £400,000 or so, had provoked awkward questions. 'What does she do with it?' one pamphleteer had asked. Republicanism, though really still a negligible force, had enjoyed a disquieting boom and Gladstone referred in 1872 to 'this great crisis of royalty'. In his rough way he revered the Queen who loathed him in return, stonewalling all his efforts to coax her out into the sunlight or to agree to discuss useful employment for the Prince of Wales. She was a little jealous of her son and his wife, who, because of her own seclusion, had assumed many of the drearier chores of royalty. The Prince and Princess of Wales became the only possible recipients for that brand of popular applause generated by the laying of foundation-stones and the opening of bazaars. It was largely due to the Prince, already developing through necessity the tact for which he was later famous, that she was infused with any enthusiasm for the Jubilee at all. In early January he presented her with a Jubilee inkstand, an elaborate affair with a crown forming the lid which, when opened, revealed a portrait of the Queen herself. 'Very pretty and useful' she noted. Not so favourable was the reaction of the colonies when asked by the Prince to contribute to the proposed Imperial Institute and even English donors were sceptical of its viability. One section of the population not slow in stoking up Jubilee fervour were the manufacturers who cudgelled their brains to produce bizarre offerings that included a walking stick made from 10,000 compressed postage stamps and a patent musical bustle that played the National Anthem whenever the wearer sat down.

Although in 1887 the Queen could look back on a quarter of a century of her own placid withdrawal, her country, like the other great nations of Europe, had been experiencing the convulsive effects of advanced industrialisation. It had produced over the years, not only an imbalance between the developed and the undeveloped nations of the world, but a marked alteration in the relative strengths of the old Great Powers. A prolonged economic depression, fiercer commercial competition and later, tariff barriers, provided a strong inducement to wield these new strengths to advantage overseas. A new world had arrived and even perceptive observers were at a loss to define exactly why: 'I do not know the cause of this sudden revolution' said Lord Salisbury. 'but there it is'.

Partly the cause and partly the result of this swift expansion was a new and convenient doctrine known as neo-mercantilism; It taught that an industrial nation required a colonial empire dependant upon it which would form a self-sufficient unit, shielded by tariffs if necessary. The colonies would send the mother country foodstuffs and raw materials in exchange for manufactured goods. If as an ecomonic argument it was fallacious, its appeal was irresistable. From the 1870s onwards it won over an increasingly large number of influential disciples and was still a force in England in the 1930s.

The confidence of the great colonial powers in their ability to control the vast tracts of land they were carving out for themselves at the time of the Golden Jubilee lay not merely in trade but in a vast export of manpower to populate and administer the new lands; this would ensure continued control by a cadre sympathetic to the intentions of the rulers at home. Advocates of the Imperial doctrine assumed, incorrectly as it turned out, that the white colonies and dominions would subordinate their individual identities to the intoxicating concept of 'a vast English nation', an Anglo-Saxon 'Great Britain'. In the second half of the nineteenth century, there grew up a firm if unstatutory assumption that the white races of the earth were destined to rule it. A young Englishman meeting Cecil Rhodes at a London Dinner party, was told 'Young man, you have been born an Englishman; as such you have won first prize in the lottery of life'.

Imperialism is thought of today as the political expression of racialism, Undeniably its main constituent was white self-aggrandisement. There was at this stage little or no intention to educate coloured populations with a view to eventual political independence. But in a world as yet unashamed by the perversions of Nazism, who could blame the European nations for feeling that the success of their civilisations had been proved in the social and material benefits brought to their own peoples by the blessings of their various systems of government? The Victorians believed that good government was more important than self-government as firmly as many believe the opposite today, and administrators and missionaries left Britain in their thousands to bring these blessings to the peoples of the Empire. By and large these exports were honest, industrious, and high-minded and achieved prodigious feats in difficult circumstances. The result was to Victorian minds, a satisfying blend of profit and social and spiritual improvement.

By 1887 the greater part of Englands imperial expansion was already complete. To India, Canada and Australia were added British East Africa in 1866, Cyprus in 1878, Borneo in 1881, Nigeria in

1885, and Burma, at the stroke of Lord Dufferin's pen, in 1886. The most emotive imperial entanglement of the century occured just before the Golden Jubilee and provides a neat example not only of contemporary attitudes but of the way in which retention of overseas interests necessitated deeper and deeper involvement.

In 1875 Disraeli had scooped financial control of the Suez Canal from under France's nose and in doing so had provoked warnings of dire consequences from Gladstone, the Liberal leader and Imperialism's most forceful opponent. The Liberal party had championed underdogs throughout the century and in recent years their leader had denounced in turn the Queen's new title of Empress of India, the Zulu War and two Afghan Wars. 'Remember' he had thundered to the electors fo Midlothian, 'that the sanctity of life in the hill villages of Afghanistan is as inviolable in the eyes of Almighty God ... as can be your own'. He detested with absolute sincerity the use of British or any power for its own ends in the subjugation of smaller nations; it was to him quite simply evil. The Queen did not agree: 'If we are to maintain our position as a first rate power ... we must with our Indian Empire and large colonies, be prepared for attacks and wars somewhere or other, continually. The true economy is to be always ready'.

In 1882, a year after Disraeli's death, the new investment was threatened by unrest in Egypt; the Cabinet despatched an army and Egypt was occupied, temporarily, it was hoped. At the same time, the Sudan had rebelled against Egyptian rule and the Liberal government was faced with the choice of further conquest or evacuation. Gladstone who had loathed the whole business from the start plumped for evacuation. General Gordon, appointed to command the operation, delayed obeying orders and was besieged; the Government delayed and Gordon was butchered. The luckless Gladstone was blamed as the murderer of a British hero and a traitor to the cause of British prestige. In the meantime trade followed the flag and Sir Evelyn Baring's administration raised Egypt from insolvency to partial prosperity.

Early in 1887 England began to prepare for the great Jubilee party. In February the Times announced 'that one hundred debtors had been set free, their liabilities being discharged by the government'. In March the Queen was asked what should be done with the surplus of the Woman's Jubilee Gift, amounting to £75,000; after much wrangling it went to found the Queen's Jubilee Nursing Institute. In April the Queen attended a concert at the Albert Hall. Lord Frederic Hamilton was struck by her inimitable dignity and by the tremendous ovation she received. 'No one who saw it can ever forget how the little old lady advanced to the front of her box and made two low sweeping curtsies to the right and to the left of her ... as she smiled through her tears on the audience in acknowledgement of the thunders of applause that greeted her.'

The celebrations began in earnest on June 20th. The Queen had breakfasted under the trees at Frogmore before driving through the day's first cheering crowds to Windsor Station where she boarded the train for Paddington. They thickened as she drove through Hyde Park, her glance perhaps straying over the smiling faces and waving hats to the great Gothic Temple enshrining the memory of the man she still missed so much. That evening she wrote in her diary: 'The day has come and I am alone'; the old, dull ache was never far away. Massed for lunch had been fifty royal and serene highnesses, 'a large family party' in which she was seated between two kings and opposite a third. 'At length feeling very tired I slipped away.'

Next day she drove in procession to Westminster Abbey for the official Thanksgiving Service but gave way to a fit of weeping before she could nerve herself to set forth. She had rejected outright the suggestions of the glass coach and the Robes of State, despite frantic pleas from her ministers and family who had hoped for some visible magnificence. In the procession were thirty-two princes

of the Queen's own house. To an Abbey spectator she was a curiously impressive sight moving slowly up the aisle, a solitary little figure in black satin after all the Robes and uniforms and jewels. And he observed, 'how right she was to come like that ... she was mother and mother-in-law and grandmother of all that regal company and there she was, a little old lady coming to church to thank God for the long years in which she had ruled her people'.

Writing to the Archbishop of Canterbury before the Service, the Queen had stipulated that it be short 'for the weather will probably be hot and the Queen feels faint if it is hot'. Bearing in mind her age and stoutness, her stamina was remarkable, but when, as on this day, her clothes included layers of silken underclothes beneath black satin, it is scarcely surprising that heat became a constant preoccupation.

As the choir sang her husband's Te Deum, she must have recalled how he had played it to her on the organ at Windsor years before. At the end of the service the royals filed past the Queen who was seated on King Edward I's Coronation chair draped with the Robes of State. Discarding protocol, the Queen embraced them all, with an extra long and affectionate clasp for her favourite daughter Vicky, Crown Princess of Germany, who had come to London with her husband not solely for the Jubilee but also to consult doctors about the hoarseness in his throat. Within a year he would have succeeded his father and died of cancer, leaving Wilhelm, Englands future enemy, as Kaiser.

It was nearly three o'clock when the Queen returned to Buckingham Palace, but before sitting down to lunch, she distributed presents – brooches to the princesses and stockpins to the princes. Afterwards she witnessed a march past of the naval guard of honour and received presents in the ballroom. 'I felt quite exhausted and ready to faint so I got into my rolling-chair and was rolled back to my room'. She lay on her bedroom sofa opening telegrams until it was time to change for the Jubilee Banquet, into a dress embroidered with roses, thistles and shamrocks in silver and diamonds. After dinner for 64, the Indian princes and the Corps Diplomatique filed by her and then 'half dead with fatigue' she was again wheeled away to her room from where she watched the illuminations.

The following day it all began again. After driving to St. James's Palace to visit her 89 year old great-aunt, the Duchess of Cambridge, she hosted another big luncheon party at Buckingham Palace where she gave Jubilee medals to the Kings and received presents. In the afternoon she drove to Hyde Park where a huge Jamboree was given for 26,000 schoolchildren. Each child received a mug with the Queens portrait on it, a bun and a glass of milk. Six military bands provided light music and a large balloon on which was painted 'Victoria' was cut loose and floated heavenwards.

In the evening she left for Windsor: another address, another statue to be unveiled, more bands, more crowds. Towards the end of dinner at the Castle, a procession of Eton boys (for whom the Queen had a particular affection) entered the quadrangle bearing torches and singing college songs. She thanked the boys in her silvery voice and was cheered to the echo. In her room in the illuminated castle she drifted into an exhausted sleep.

The next four weeks involved more receptions, garden parties, a review in Hyde Park of 28,000 volunteers, the laying of a foundation stone of the still unpaid-for Imperial Institute and a party at the Albert Hall for the Battersea Dog's Home. Another review at Aldershot, a garden party at Hatfield – the home of her shrewd and gloomy Prime Minister Lord Salisbury, and a memorial stone for the Prince Consort's new statue on Smith's lawn at Windsor.

She arrived at Osborne on the verge of collapse. Still there was the fleet to be reviewed at Spithead – 135 ships and 20,000, men and afterwards a ceremonious leavetaking of the Indian Princes.

Finally it petered out and the Queen journeyed north to Balmoral. Like a shy girl before a grand party, she had been fraught with

From the supplement to the *Queen*, December 1st, 1887.

Souvenir bookmarker, 1887.

Plate commemorating Prince Albert's achievements in the arts and sciences.

Golden Jubilee cup and saucer, 1887.

The advance of travel in the Queen's reign.

above Embroidered picture celebrating the Queen's Diamond Jubilee

above left Eno's Fruit Salts 1887.

The Queen's family tree in photographs.

nerves, dreading the ceremony and the attention. And now it was over and 'all was the most perfect success'. As the memorable year of 1887 drew to a close, she wrote with pride in her diary: 'Never can I forget this brilliant year, so full of marvellous kindness, loyalty and devotion of so many millions, which really I could hardly have expected'. The Queen might reasonably have expected loyalty from the great ones of her Empire, but it was the deluge of affection from the great mass of her subjects that had the most marked effect on her. The cheering, happy crowds in the squalid purlieus on the South Bank of London, the thousands of well-wishing letters she received from the poorest of her people, often written on cheap paper in painfully formed handwriting, had, more than once, reduced her to astonished tears. What had she done to deserve all this? It was all the more surprising for on some of these well-wishers, living in the grim mining towns of the Rhondda and the smoky, industrial cities of Lancashire, the bright sun of her Empire had scarcely risen. What did they really know of her character, her sense of duty, her honesty and forthright simplicity? On one of her drives through Dublin, an old woman was heard to remark. 'Sure, and she's only an old body like ourselves'. Of the jumbled reactions that go to make up royal popularity, it was perhaps as eloquent as any.

The Golden Jubilee was certainly a turning point. To date her sense of duty, always strong, had expressed itself in an aloof and private performance with no audience to encourage and appreciate. Now, forced in front of the greatest audience she had yet faced, she was cheered not just as the Queen, but as a much loved old lady. One wonders whether she now felt badly over not having gone more among her people, but whatever the reason, when the Jubilee was over, she never again reverted to her former seclusion.

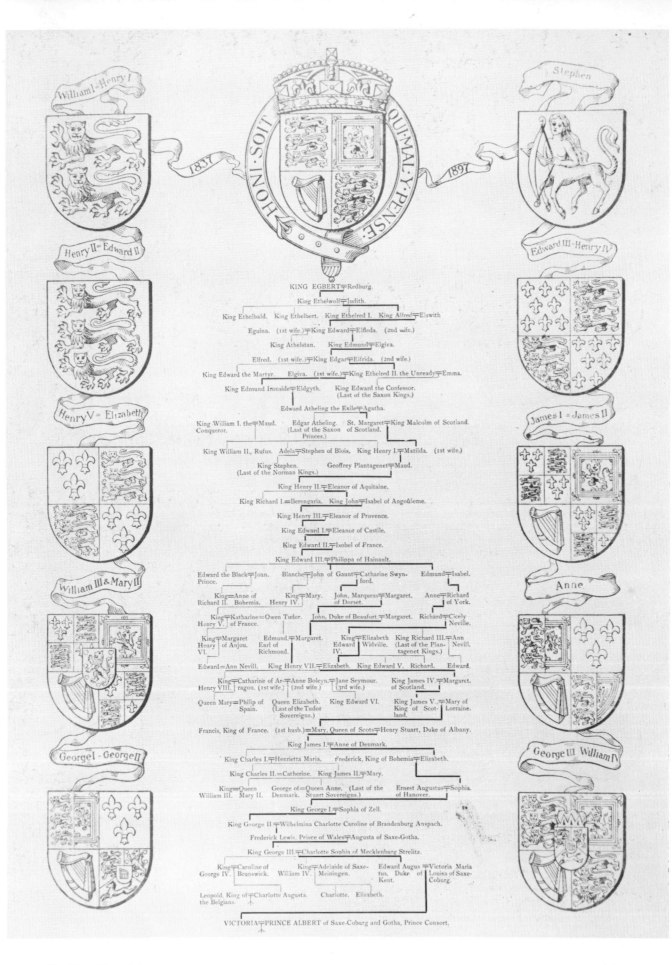

The Royal line of descent.

The Duchess of Clarence (later Queen Adelaide),
Queen Victoria's aunt by marriage.

The Duke of Clarence (later King William IV),
Queen Victoria's uncle.

The Duke of Kent, Queen Victoria's father.

The Duchess of Kent, Queen Victoria's mother.

Neither of Victoria's uncles, George IV or William IV, had legitimate sons and she succeeded as her father's only child.

Root and branch; the living descendants of Queen Victoria.

A family gathering at Coburg, April 19th, 1894 for the wedding of two of Victoria's grandchildren, Princess Victoria Melita, daughter of Prince Alfred (*back row, far right*) to the Grand Duke of Hesse. Seated from left to right are: the Kaiser Wilhelm II, Queen Victoria and the Kaiser's mother, the Empress Frederick. Behind the Kaiser stands the future Emperor Nicholas of Russia and his fiancee, (another granddaughter). Behind Nicholas stands the Prince of Wales.

THE BRITISH LION PREPARES FOR THE JUBILEE.

A ROYAL HOUSE-WARMING.

It was a question what should be done with them. There was such a lot of them. And each of them had a suite. Of course if they had come unattended, bringing only a valet or a maid, it would have been possible to put them all up at Buckingham Palace—with a little crowding. But not at all. This man had his chamberlain, that a master of the horse, or somebody. So they had to be spread over as large an area as possible.

There was not much question as to whom should be housed at Pimlico. The kings of course had the call, although some of them (for family reasons) preferred Marlborough House. The Belgians, the Portuguese, Saxony and all the Berlin contingent, with the gentleman from Vienna, had absolutely a right to reside in the Palace of Pimlico. Then there was the Italian Duke who had been a King once upon a time in Spain (he retired after he had had quite enough of it)—well, he might expect to be put up in Buckingham House. And these, with the members of "the Family" quite exhausted the accommodation in Pimlico.

Marlborough House, always hospitable, opened its doors to anyone, but especially to anyone more intimately connected with Denmark. "Only too pleased to see anybody," was the idea, but the central notion was "Denmark." Lucky *voyageurs* who got to Marlborough House. Quite sure of a very good time. Theatres, operas, everything ! A real good time ! Clarence House drew the line at Russia. In Edinburgh a bawbee *is* a bawbee, and, even when guns don't go off, a "saxpence" is sometimes capable of "banging." So the line was drawn at Russia. The inhabitants of the Wild North are no doubt an admirable race, but not too amusing. So perhaps they were a trifle *triste*. It is to be hoped, if this was indeed the case, that dark moments were chased away by fiddling, and there was some one at hand to compensate the fiddler. And, for the rest, there were hotels. One opposite Buckingham Palace, most conveniently situated. "Sleep out, and take meals in the house." That was the idea. And then there were private lodgings. So, when all is said and done, why should they not be comfortable ? Even the Siamese and other darkies were appropriately put up. Yes, and this last feat was performed without asking for accommodation at the Hall of the Moore and Burgess Minstrels !

VANITIES.

I REGRET to state that the health of the Crown Prince of Germany is in an extremely bad condition. Doctor Morel Mackenzie has been attending him, and Professor Virchow has, I am informed, now come to the conclusion that the Prince is suffering from cancer. That a very serious and dangerous operation will have to take place is now unfortunately almost certain. This operation was suggested some weeks ago, though it was opposed by Prince Bismarck for political reasons, and especially pending the formation of the new French Cabinet.

* * * * * *

The "Jubilee Juggins" won last week £7000 at cards at a Club, but the next day he lost £36,000, for which he promptly gave a cheque. I am told that at some race-meeting a few days ago he went into the ring and asked what were the odds. "Ten to one "that you will be broke before Goodwood," was the reply from one of the bookmakers.

JUBILEE GUESTS.

Lord Chamberlain. "ALL RIGHT, YOUR ROYAL HIGHNESSES. YOU'LL ALL BE ATTENDED TO IN YOUR TURNS."

above left The sudden descent of foreign royalties on London caused acute accommodation problems though the more important of them seem to have found satisfactory berths. Nineteenth century royalties, of which there were a colossal number, were obsessed with precedence and inexact observance of the ritual ruffled feathers. On one occasion the Prince of Wales was obliged to placate a mortified Crown Prince of Germany who found he had been placed behind the King of the Cannibal Islands; the Prince gave judgement: 'the man was either a King or a damned nigger' and if a King, belonged where he was.

above right To English eyes, minor foreign royalties were considered excitable and faintly ridiculous; *Punch*, always calm in a crisis, imposes a sense of order.

below left Topical jottings from *Vanity Fair*, whose concern over the German Crown Prince was justified. The 'Jubilee Juggins' referred to actually existed. He was a colourful lunatic named Benson who was addicted to gambling in any form and did indeed win and lose huge sums. On one occasion, he and some friends agreed to race cockroaches around entrée dishes; when the runners were dropped onto their individual courses, Benson's entry ran for its life – prior to the race his plate had been heated in the oven.

opposite Coverage by *Punch* of the Jubilee tempered pride with humour. The British Lion and John Bull, now, sadly, vanished figures, expressed the national sentiments of the hour to several generations of *Punch* readers. On international issues, Germany was represented by a gruff, picklehaube'd Bismarck, France by a wan maiden and the parvenu America by an intrusive and bumpkin Uncle Sam. This type of charming oversimplification died through over use in 1914 when John Bull went to the aid of 'gallant little Belgium' against 'the Hun'.

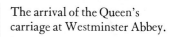

The arrival of the Queen's carriage at Westminster Abbey.

left Ellen Terry, the most celebrated and best-loved British actress of the day.

below A loyal address from the actors and managers of the leading theatrical companies. The Queen's taste in literature and the arts was limited. She liked opera and most of the prominent singers of the day performed for her. While admiring Shakespeare – 'what a man Shakespeare was' – and trying in vain to understand Goethe's *Faust*, her real favourite was Marie Corelli.

Members of the family and the household were regularly coerced into amateur theatricals with such delicious titles as 'Little Toddle kins' and 'A scrap of paper'. On a French visit, Victoria succumbed to pressure to witness, with delight, a performance by the exotic Sarah Bernhardt, over whose morals she had reservations. A vintage story concerns Bernhardt's performance of Cleopatra, when, after she had raved and staggered through her closing lines, an elderly Englishwoman turned to her companion and remarked 'How different, how very different from the home life of own dear Queen'.

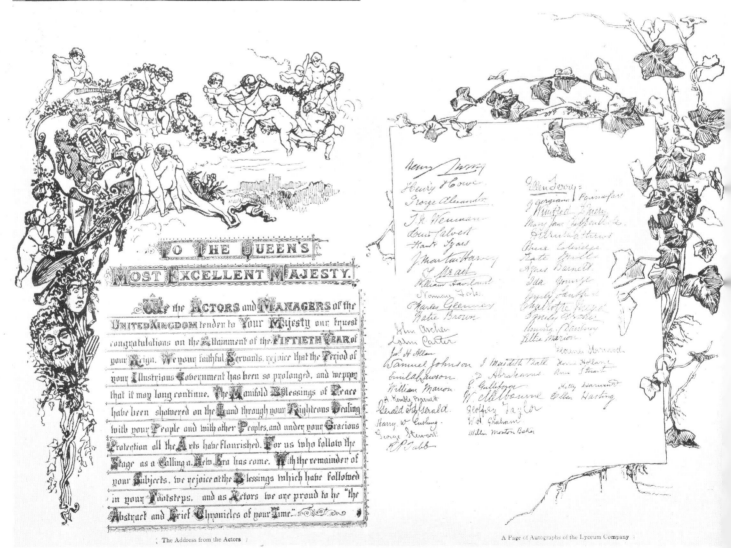

The Address from the Actors

A Page of Autographs of the Lyceum Company

above The Prince of Wales, the Queen, and the Princess of Wales photographed by Bassano in 1887. The Queen is wearing the small Imperial Crown and her wedding veil and lace flounce. The Princess had made the final attempt on behalf of the family to persuade the Queen to wear the Robes of State. She emerged from the Royal Closet, red-faced and downcast, murmuring 'I was never so snubbed in my life'. Alexandra's long neck and ample bosom might have been made for the display of jewels and the 'chokers' she popularised. The Jubilee guests at Marlborough House included Crown Prince Rudolph of Austria, and the Princess' Greek relations, but the spirits of the party were dampened by the visible suffering of the German Crown Prince. Though perhaps not to modern eyes the famed beauty she was considered then, the Princess' charm strengthened an impression of extraordinary youth. (She was then 43)

Jubilee Ode by *Punch*.

'Clang bells, cheer Britons, clamour voices sweet
Of English womanhood in chorus clear.
Flood with a sea of faces the grey street
Of Babylon the drear!
The flower-pied meadow-world is scarce more gay
Than the thronged city vistas on this festal day.'

right The Queen arrives at a Jubilee treat for 26,000 children in Hyde Park given by the *Daily Telegraph*. At the end of the Party, the hot air balloon, on which was painted 'VICTORIA' was released, and one child, doubtless fuddled by the gaiety, exclaimed 'O look! there's the Queen going up to heaven'.

The long road at the top of the picture is the Bayswater Road, a few miles north of which was still a rural area. Park Lane was not yet the grandiose boulevard it would become at the turn of the century, and the Marble Arch, now marooned in a maelstrom of rushing traffic, was the pedestrian entrance to Hyde Park. No doubt the Forsyte sisters spent the evening at their home in Bayswater Road, teetering at the noise and music, while James Forsyte grumbled from his window in Park Lane.

THE JUBILEE YACHT-RACE, for which the Prince of Wales started a number of our best yachts from Gravesend on Wednesday, the Fifteenth of June, and the course of which is round the coasts of Great Britain and Ireland, has naturally greatly occupied the attention of dwellers in the seaports which calculated on obtaining glimpses of the white-winged clippers. The Thistle was conspicuous by her absence. But most of the other famous yachts are competing.

A telegram from Lloyd's signal station at Dunnet Head, dated 8.45 on Monday morning, says:—Selene passed 11.47 a.m. yesterday. Aline passed 12.2 p.m. yesterday. Selene about one mile ahead of Aline. Gwendoline passed 10.57 p.m. yesterday, about nine miles astern of Aline. Bridesmaid passed at 2.20 a.m. to-day. All well. Wind N.W. Light clear. Sea smooth. A second telegram from Dunnet Head, timed 1.5 p.m. on Monday, reports:—Atlantis yacht passed at 12.25 p.m. All well. Bound west.

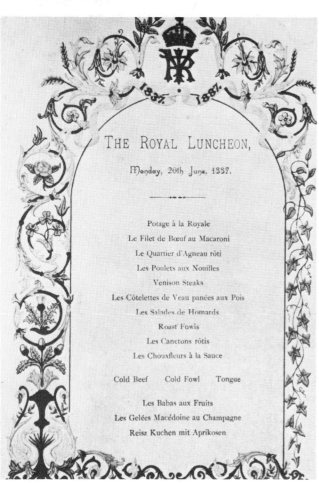

THE ROYAL LUNCHEON,

Monday, 20th June, 1887.

Potage à la Royale

Le Filet de Bœuf au Macaroni

Le Quartier d'Agneau rôti

Les Poulets aux Nouilles

Venison Steaks

Les Côtelettes de Veau panées aux Pois

Les Salades de Homards

Roast Fowls

Les Canetons rôtis

Les Chouxfleurs à la Sauce

Cold Beef   Cold Fowl   Tongue

Les Babas aux Fruits

Les Gelées Macédoine au Champagne

Reisz Kuchen mit Aprikosen

left Luncheon for the visiting royalties at Buckingham Palace; though not a large menu for the time, it is none the less formidable to calorie-conscious modern eyes. The Queen liked highly flavoured food and wine in moderation. She was naturally inclined to corpulence and in her youth attempted numerous diets – all in vain. She took little exercise and disliked doing so; in later years those father figures like Melbourne who had counselled walking, were long dead. In her closing years, despite a rotund appearance, she lost weight; when her sons lifted her into her coffin, they were astonished at her lightness.

below The Golden Jubilee Procession, June 21st, 1887. The Royal carriage passing the Treasury on the return to Buckingham Palace after the service at Westminster Abbey. The Queen is smiling broadly.

opposite right The Queen posed for this photograph at Osborne two months after the Jubilee in the dress she wore for the procession. Much of the Queen's powerful aura stemmed from her unique appearance. Black satin, lace, diamonds, plump white hands, hooded eyes and the little beak nose surmounted by the special Jubilee bonnet; weary resignation and a kind of dowdy magnificence added up to the quintessence of a forthright old grandmother.

VICTORIA
ALL NATIONS SALUTE YOU

above Street decorations in Lower Regent Street seen from Piccadilly Circus. The ingenuity and richness of Victorian Jubilee Street decorations, which were all made by hand, put London's recent efforts in the shade. Apart from economics, it was perhaps due to the fact that Mayfair and the West End were then the exclusive territory of a prosperous society of which the Monarchy formed the obvious head.

To the left of the picture stands the Criterion Bar, a visit to which was a ritual pleasure dreamt of by Englishmen on overseas service in the colonies. At the bottom centre of the picture, an intrepid pedestrian negotiates the traffic. On the right stands Messrs Drew's premises where you could buy leather and other luxury personal goods of a quality unknown today.

opposite and overleaf The social calendar of the Jubilee would have been pored over by those to whom the doings of the great and famous were a source of fascination and envy. The reference to an earlier Jubilee is an error; in 1809, King George III though increasingly insane, was still king; George IV, soon to be Regent reigned only ten years.

The Tichborne case convulsed society for several years. The eldest son was lost at sea, presumed drowned, and 'the unfortunate nobleman' succeeded as Baronet. Then, from darkest Australia, appeared a claimant, who was authenticated by old Lady Tichborne. But Victorian society, ever vigilant in the defence of property, closed ranks and the claimant lost his case.

Lady Revelstoke's house in Charles Street is now the English-Speaking Union and Sir George Wombwell was a veteran of Balaclava.

Since the burden of entertaining foreign royalties fell on the Royal Purse, rich court families, like the Cadogans and Rothschilds with large London establishments, were frequently requested by the Crown to help out. King Edward VII understood very well this aspect of royal patronage and extracted full advantage from it.

IN SOCIETY.

LET us peacefully digest the comforting reflection—the J*b*l*e is past. Kings and Queens have shuffled themselves off, and even the very knaves are played out. But the Cowboys and the "first families" we still have with us. This, too, is consoling. The sawdust, the hammering, the mobs of loyal but disreputable-looking people, with their villainous tobacco, all crowded together into one short week, have given me a serious attack of Jubilee Jumps, which will certainly spare me from ever having to go a second time through similar horrors. I hear that one old lady looked out at the procession on Tuesday from the identical window in Cockspur Street through which nearly eighty years back she witnessed the Jubilee of George IV.! This poor lady has been sorely tried, and I can only hope that the joys of the next world may in some degree compensate her for her troubles of this one.

However, now that we can breathe, I freely admit it has been a brilliant and extraordinary success, and every possible praise is due on our part to those whose management and energy have brought this about. Sir Charles Warren and the Duke of Portland deserve well of their country, for they have literally done wonders. Two millions of people spread for twenty-four weary hours along a two-mile route, and not a single case before the magistrates the next morning! Downright enthusiasm. As to the police, they did their work splendidly, with wonderful tact and good temper, and to this no small part of the success achieved is due. I sincerely hope the public in general will come forward handsomely to recognise their services. The admirable and almost incredible behaviour of all concerned is the best tribute her loyal people can offer to a good Queen in celebration of fifty years' beneficent rule. To quote one of the commonest and most appropriate inscriptions, our Queen is truly

"A blessing to the nation, and by the nation blessed."

For all that, I am still suffering from acute Jubilee Jumps, and nothing but "largess" will cure me. Besides, I fully expected to see the Grand Old Muddler's head borne on a pole in front of the show. By some oversight, probably, this was omitted, but I have no doubt now that, attention being called to it, an early opportunity will be seized to carry this out.

By the way, I do not vouch for the truth of the following in every sense but one. Sir William Harcourt the other day asked the G.O.M. how he spelt the word Jubilee. With that supernatural seriousness which is his chief characteristic, he immediately and laboriously spelt out the letters "J U B I—"

"No, no," cried Sir William; "it is J B L double E, U and I "are out of it." Mr. Gladstone is a cross between a Bishop, a pedagogue, and a middle-class tradesman.

In the flurry and excitement of the Jubilee, the coming of age of "the unfortunate nobleman," Sir Henry Doughty Tichborne, which was celebrated last week at Tichborne Park, has been entirely overlooked. However, it was a very brilliant affair, and a pleasant ending to the sensational events of some ten years back. The "house party" included Sir Percy and Lady Radcliffe, Mrs. and Miss Silvertop, Mrs. Carrington Smythe, and innumerable Arundells and Petres; whilst at Brookwood were gathered for the event Mrs. and the Misses Towneley, Miss Tempest, Mrs. Herbert Dormer, and last, though by no means least, the future Lady Tichborne, Miss Gwendoline Petre. On Monday the sports in the park were spoilt by the fall of one of the acrobats, which unfortunately resulted fatally. The county ball took place in the evening. On Tuesday there were the tenants' dinner and ball and the fireworks, and on Wednesday there was a further continuation of the same programme. Thus, what with coming of age, coming into a large fortune, and becoming a benedict, the "unfortunate nobleman" might fairly be rechristened the fortunate one.

Thursday, the 16th.—These last ten days we have been playing exclusively with Court cards. At Sir George Wombwell's dance there were seventeen present, which being one too many, I conclude he must have had one up his sleeve. There was however far too great a crush to detect whether the play was quite fair; and as I lost nothing, I will not grumble.

Friday, the 17th.—The Duc d'Aumale in the evening had a particularly good hand, holding almost all the Court cards at present in England. The party invited to meet him was exceedingly small, only about seventy having been asked. Lady Elizabeth Biddulph received the guests. The Duc d'Aumale bought last year Montcorvo House in Ennismore Gardens, formerly well-known when in the hands of Mr. Albert Sandeman. It is now literally crammed with beautiful pictures, amongst the most noticeable being the "Vierge de la Maison d'Orleans" by Raphael, and Gerard's famous portrait of Napoleon I.

Later Lady Revelstoke gave her third dance in Charles Street. This was small but not uneventful, as it was on this occasion that the popular "Bobby" Spencer and Miss Baring, the second daughter of the house, agreed to join their future fates together.

Lady Tenterden's reception in Portland Place was very pleasant and diplomatic, whilst numerous Ribbons and Stars foreshadowed the coming J*b*l*e.

Mrs. Pereira's dance in Park Lane was a singular success, though some disappointment was felt that no picture cards turned up. I cannot see what particular pleasure people can have in being in the same room with Royalties. For my part, I always feel happier and freer when they are absent. Evidently we are not all agreed on this point.

Mrs. Riddell's dance in Ennismore Gardens was very Catholic and Apostolic, but at the same time exceedingly pleasant. Being Friday, we all waited till past twelve before once again returning to the fascinations of a meat diet.

The Russian Embassy monopolised the Grand Duke and Duchess Serge of Russia for the evening, and after having dined them well, the diplomats of all nations were bidden to Madame de Staal's, to pay their humble respects. They came too in their numbers, tall and short, fat and thin, alike bending their bodies and attitudinising, as is their wont. It was pretty. Monsieur de Staal is out and away the most popular Ambassador in London, as he is the most genial and the kindliest of chiefs, and the Russian Embassy never attempts anything which it cannot do regally.

Saturday, the 18th.—This time the picture cards were held by Countess Károlyi, who entertained the Crown Prince Rudolph of Austria and, amongst others, the Duke of Cambridge and Princess Mary and the Duke of Teck. The rooms were entirely decorated with roses, and the general effect was charming. One individual wore a wondrous star, and many speculated as to what it signified. The quotation, "Twinkle, twinkle, little star, "How I wonder what you are," was in common use. As yet the mystery remains unsolved.

The reception at the Siamese Legation was a motley gathering of every hue and every shade. The Queen of the Sandwich Islands—it has quite the ring of a railway buffet—was the guest of the evening, and Prince Christian represented the English Royalty.

By the way, so the story goes, when staying with a certain provincial Dean, Prince and Princess Christian rather outstayed their expected time. It was however their practice daily to attend the morning service; so, to give them a gentle hint, the choir were instructed one day on their entering the Cathedral to strike up, "Onward, Christians, onward go." The plan met with complete success.

The Gallery Club in the evening gave their first At Home to ladies, at the Grosvenor Gallery. This was all it merited to be, for not only was first-rate music provided, but throughout the night there was ample room for all to enjoy it in perfect comfort; and strawberries and cream, though in the morning selling at no less a price than a sovereign a pound first hand, were plentiful.

The Park on Saturday evening was a sight certainly, but a peculiar one. Everybody seemed to have decided that they would drive out and see the Royalties. The result was a dense mass of jobmasters' stock, with here and there a " chawriot " struggling to be free. Hyde Park Corner presented an impenetrable jungle of country cousins, interlacing queues of carriages, islands of stragglers in imminent death from wheel or hoof, vociferating policemen, titupping horses, and Volunteer bands, with a *soupçon* of Jubilee language. "How many Royalties are " there out ? " inquired I, with perforce breathless excitement, of a policeman. "Ony a couple of Zulus, Sir, and there's no " knowin' who *they* are."

Sunday, the 19th.—The Park has become entirely hopeless. Over 12,000 people paid for chairs between sunrise and sunset, whilst in the afternoon Kings, cowboys, and washerwomen's carts loaded with dirty children drove up and down the drive.

Our old friend " Butterfly Bill," as the President of the Society of British Artists has been irreverently christened, received in Suffolk Street. The people were delightful, the dress outrageous, the heat suffocating—without in the least intending a pun—and the pictures "amazing." However, anything given under. the auspices of that very popular and eccentric artist, Mr. Whistler, is bound to be a success, and this particular function was in no way an exception to the rule. As I do not

A JUBILEE PRIVATE VIEW.
(Turning an Honest Penny-a-Line.)

The Duchess of Dilwater (Art-Critic to the South Pentonville Gazette) writes in her Note-book :—" THE FUNDAMENTAL THEME OR LEIT-MOTIF OF MR. SOAPLEY'S EXQUISITE PORTRAIT OF MRS. BLAZER, IS AN IMPASSIONED *ADAGIO* IN THE MINOR KEY OF BLUE, TENDERLY EMBROIDERED WITH A SUB-DOMINANT FUGUE IN GREEN AND GRAY AND GOLD !" &c., &c.

Lady Slangboro (Purveyor of Social pars to the Bermondsey Figaro) :—" IT'S ALL TOMMY ROT ABOUT THE DUCHESS OF DILWATER NOT BEING ON SPEAKING TERMS WITH HER LEARY OLD BLOKE OF A SPOUSE. BOTH THEIR GRACES WERE PRESENT, DARBY-AND-JOANING IT ALL OVER THE SHOP." &c., &c.

Viscountess Crewelstown (who does the Fashions for the Barnes and Putney Express) :—" LADY SLANGBORO WAS THERE, LOOKING LOVELY IN A RICH SALMON ÉCRU POULT DE SOIE MATELOTTE RUCHÉE À LA BARIGOULE, WITH POINTES D'ESTRAGON PANACHÉ, AND BOUILLON-AISES OF THON MARINÉ EN JARDINIÈRE, FROM MADAM ALDEGONDE'S (719, PICCADILLY)." &c., &c.

above In a leisured age which gave time to many men and women to occupy themselves with just looking their best, it was scarcely surprising that Oscar Wilde's Lord Henry Wotton pondered over whether, at a Royal Academy View, it was more important to see the pictures or the people.

opposite Social 'lions' from abroad were swiftly ensnared by hostesses for display at receptions, of which there would probably have been two or three every night of the season and at which everybody saw everybody they had been seeing all summer; most of these pasty maidens and monocled men of fashion did little else all year round.

OUR DRAWING-ROOM PETS.

(*We give the Colonies a Turn.*)

KANGAROO JIM, THE CHAMPION AUSTRALIAN BOOMERANG-THROWER, IS RAPIDLY BECOMING THE IDOL OF OUR MOST EXCLUSIVE LONDON CIRCLES (TO THE INTENSE AMUSEMENT OF HIS NATIVE MELBOURNE, WHERE HE IS ONLY KNOWN TO SOCIETY IN HIS PUBLIC CAPACITY OF PROFESSIONAL STREET ACROBAT.)

N.B.—KANGAROO JIM'S ADVENTUROUS YOUTH WAS SPENT IN THE COOKABOO ISLANDS, AND HE OWNS TO HAVING FREQUENTLY PARTAKEN OF ROAST MISSIONARY THERE; INDEED HE DESCRIBES THESE BANQUETS WITH INIMITABLE GUSTO, AND SEEMS NOT A LITTLE PROUD OF HIS CULINARY SKILL.

wish him however to make an "arrangement in black and blue" of me, I will say no more.

Monday, the 20th.—All the Kings and Queens, led by the Prince and Princess of Wales, went early to Buffalo Bill, who provided a special morning performance for their benefit. But "Oh! what "a surprise!" When the Deadwood Coach came on the ground, the Princess and two Kings courageously stepped into it, and were duly attacked by Red Shirt and his tribe, and again duly rescued by the gallant cowboys. When will wonders cease? Was it intended as an undress rehearsal of what might occur the following day? The poor Czar should really have been of the party, so as to have given his experience as to the realistic effect produced. Afterwards Buffalo Bill was presented to, and shook hands with, each of the Royalties, which adds one more event to his already eventful career.

Mr. Hamilton Aidé—who has written songs and sung them, written books and read them, composed poetry, stayed at Sandringham, and done many other recordable things—gave a tea.

Tuesday, the 21st.—The J*b*l*e. By seven o'clock the whole town was astir, and by half-past eight nearly every available stand and seat was occupied. At half-past ten, when the first procession, composed of Indian Princes and Oriental notables,

arrived in Piccadilly, the street was choked from end to end with carriages of all sorts and descriptions. After a delay of some twenty minutes however, these gradually melted away, and then the pageant began. The procession to the Abbey was too disjointed to be impressive, and the Queen looked scared and ill-tempered; but the return journey was one of the finest sights that have ever been produced. Coming down Piccadilly hill, it looked like a fine stream of gold, whilst here and there the glitter of the swords and decorations appeared like a refreshing spray from the waters. The Duke of Portland, in a gorgeous uniform which he had designed for himself, leading the line, was simply magnificent, and, with the Crown Prince of Germany, easily divided the honours of the day. The latter, with his white uniform, barbaric helmet, and Marshal's báton, looked statuesque, and was received with enthusiasm. The Duchess of Albany, with her eyes sparkling with pleasure, accompanying every bow with a pretty smile, fascinated all. The other Royalties were too automatic in their recognition of the crowd.

As to the Queen, she was crying and laughing by turns, and was delighted with the marvellous reception she had received along the whole route. Never was there such a success. The Duke of Portland, as Master of the Horse, did his work to perfection. No country could have turned out a finer lot of horses or a better appointed set of carriages. Only three slight hitches occurred. Soon after leaving Buckingham Palace, going up Constitution Hill, Lord Lorne's horse reared, and rid himself of his kilted burden. I understand this mishap was entirely Lord Lorne's own fault, as the Duke of Westminster had offered him a quiet, though less showy, horse, which he declined. The quiet smile his brothers-in-law retained during the remainder of the route is quite inexplicable, seeing the acute pain the occurrence must have caused them. Again, in Waterloo Place, one of the horses in the Duke of Aosta's carriage got his leg over the trace, and the Duke and other occupants had to dismount, and the procession stop, till this had been remedied. The last and most serious hitch was on the return from the Abbey, when, by some inadvertence, the police in Pall Mall neglected to keep the road clear for the Indian Princes. Two of these were so infuriated that they got down from their carriages and walked home. It was a pity likewise that the Duke of Portland forgot to supervise this part of the *cortège*, as some of the carriages which contained the Oriental contingent were positively miserable. However, the £20,000 which is said to have passed through his hands for the occasion was certainly most judiciously spent, and a finer pageant has never been seen. Of course, in a procession of this peaceful kind there is never that compressed sense of power which is produced by an Emperor at the head of his troops, or such reviews as were occasionally held under the Empire; but in its way it was a thing well worthy of the nation. The Queen met with a most enthusiastic reception throughout, and the behaviour of the people themselves has fairly astonished everybody. By the way, I hear the cost of entertaining the Royalties is over £1500 a-day, which entirely comes out of Her Majesty's privy purse.

One omission was regrettable, and that was the total want of music. Full military bands should have preceded every procession. Also it was a pity that the resources of the Royal Stables rendered it impossible to put the numerous foreign crowned heads in open carriages.

In the Abbey the most theatrical incident was provided by Nature, as a thin ray of sunlight, glancing past the Queen, fell directly on the effigies of past Sovereigns that lay peacefully behind her.

The illuminations at night were fine, but they lacked that continuity and regularity which are such a feature of similar foreign fêtes. Eaton Place was particularly good, being uniform, and having been entirely superintended by the Duke of Athole. So also was part of Wigmore Street, the Bank of England, and the branch bank in Burlington Gardens, Messrs. Pears and Co. in Oxford Street, Poole's, Peter Robinson's, Busvine's, and the block of buildings fronting Grosvenor Place. The gardens of St. James's Square were also prettily arranged with Chinese lanterns. As to the decorations, they were mostly of a very flimsy character. Lady Burdett-Coutts's was elaborate, but scarcely agreeable; and Lady Borthwick's house, entirely garlanded with flowers, was very good. But money had been more freely used in putting up remunerative stands than expended over unremunerative decorations. Lord Rothschild's house was certainly however an exception. Apsley House was hardly as successful.

In the evening the Queen gave a large Royal dinner-party, and later about three hundred guests, mostly *chefs de Mission* and officers of State, were invited. The Queen received the guests in person, standing at the door of the big drawing-room. All Her Majesty's presents were exposed, as also were the masses of flowers that had been sent her from all parts of the country. A crown six feet high, and a silver corbeille filled with red roses, the gift of Lord Rothschild, were particularly admired. And so ended the Jubilee.

Wednesday, the 22nd.—One of the most graceful of the Jubilee fêtes occurred to-day, and is entirely due for its origin and success to Mr. Edward Lawson. Thirty thousand children were feasted in Hyde Park, and all the Royalties in London attended. The Park was divided into three sections—1st, "between the lines," for society at large, to which admission was obtained by ticket; 2nd, the space kept by the Guards and the police for the children, for which special tickets were issued; and 3rd, an inner Holy of Holies, reserved for the Royal guests and the favoured few who were asked to meet them. This enclosure however was finally broken into before Her Majesty arrived, which she did very late. Miss Dunn, a young lady who has never missed attendance at school for seven years, was the heroine of the hour, and very unhappy the poor child looked when pushed to the front. She was presented with a Jubilee Jug by the Queen, who by the way did *not* perpetrate a pun and say, "Well *done*!" One poor child broke her mug, and was so sorely distressed that attention was called to her. However, when asked what she held in her handkerchief, she replied, "I've got the Queen all "right;" and I am happy to say she is to be given another in its stead.

Lord Cadogan has been accorded the privilege of welcoming at his table the largest number of actual and future Sovereigns ever known, at least during our generation. The Jubilee was unlucky in so far as regards the number of large representative establishments of the aristocracy of England open for hospitality and festivity, and Chelsea House was the only available *point d'appui* for our foreign guests to refresh themselves before paying a visit to the Foreign Office. The accommodation in the dining-room being insufficient, the guests were entertained in the drawing-rooms, dinner being served in the ball-room. A special staircase was built outside, leading down into the kitchens from the side windows; and, in point of fact, nothing was left undone to ensure perfect comfort and to make this gigantic effort a success. Four reigning Monarchs, ten Crown and Hereditary Princes and Princesses, and the whole of our own Royal Family, with the exception, of course, of the Queen, honoured Lord Cadogan with their presence.

The Foreign Office was a terrible crush, and the band was constantly interrupted by having to strike up "God Save the "Queen" as some fresh Royalty appeared. Still it was a brilliant scene, as red coats were *de rigueur*.

Mrs. Menzies' dance in Carlton House Terrace was a great success. The Blue Hungarian Band played to perfection, and the rooms were entirely decorated with roses. The floor this time was far better, and it was rumoured that a new one had been put down for the occasion. Kooch Behar, who came on from the Foreign Office, was an amiable Othello, with whom many Desdemonas danced vigorously and continuously.

By the way, in going, I heard a woman inquire what the letters V.R. meant. "Very Respectable," was the ready answer.

The Hungarian Ball, though for a short while patronised by Royalty, was scarcely the success it should have been; whilst Lady Goldsmid's reception in Piccadilly, though difficult to get at, well rewarded the efforts of those who reached it safely.

I hear that the India Office have had considerable difficulty in restraining one Oriental potentate from bringing over his whole harem.

Friday, 24th June, 1887.

AFTER THE JUBILEE.

BRITISH LION (*rather limp*). "WELL, IT HAS BEEN A SPLENDID SUCCESS!! AND NOW—A—WE MUST REALLY
GET *BACK TO BUSINESS!!!*"

Business included the second reading of the Irish Land Bill in the Commons, a major row over charges against Parnell printed in *The Times*, and the arrest of an M.P. for 'resisting and assaulting the police' when the Socialists and unemployed tried to assemble in Trafalgar Square. A proclamation had forbidden public meetings and the Guards had been called out.

Queen Victoria with the children of her third son: Prince Arthur and Princess Margaret of Connaught *circa* 1885. 'I love to hear the little feet and merry voices above' she wrote. Daisy Connaught was uncontrollable but was indulged by the Queen because she was so 'funny'.

opposite above The visit of the Russian Emperor to Balmoral 1896. Left to right: Ghillie, Duke of Connaught, the Emperor, Princess Patricia of Connaught, the Queen, Princess Helena Victoria of Schleswig-Holstein, the Empress, Duchess of Connaught and Princess Margaret of Connaught. On her deathbed, the Queen would ask for her Pomeranian 'Turi' seen here on her lap.

opposite below The Queen at breakfast with Princess Henry of Battenberg and Princess Helena Victoria of Schleswig-Holstein (*facing camera*) at Nice 1895. The Aga Khan, staying in the same hotel, described her Indian servants as 'distinctly second class'. After 1895 the Queen was lent a private villa which is probably where this photograph was taken. She always took about a hundred servants with her, and when in England, breakfasted off a service of solid gold.

above right Queen Victoria lunching with her Battenberg grandchildren.

below right Tea at Osborne. Neither of the Indian servants here are the famous Munshi for, after his promotion to the rank of 'gentleman', all photographs of him waiting at table were destroyed. Stupid and pushy, he survived numerous household plots to dislodge him until finally they threatened to resign *en masse* at the suggestion that he should eat with them during a foreign visit. Eventually, he overplayed his hand and his influence was curbed.

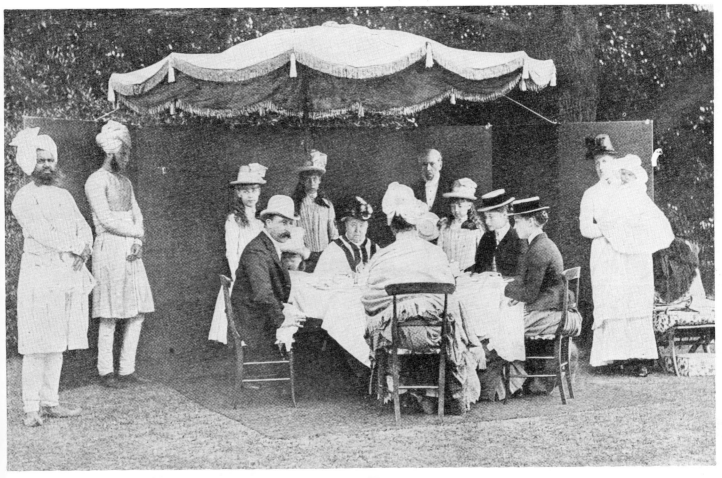

'The domestic shrine of beauty and refinement' – the drawing-room at Osborne in the Isle of Wight photographed in 1885. The house had been built to the designs of the Prince Consort in the style of a Florentine palazzo. Osborne was one of many attempts made by the Queen in her life to escape from the grandiose to the snug but the new house grew and grew till the charm which had initially attracted her had vanished. The rooms, compared with Windsor and Buckingham Palace, were small and the decoration was purely mid-Victorian.

The drawing room was L-shaped which held advantages for the household since it meant that when one was in the further half of the room, one was not strictly 'in the presence'; there were evenings in the Queen's later years when she was silent and preoccupied and conversation was held in low tones amid an atmosphere of general gloom. Lord Rosebery said that he thought this room was the ugliest room in the world, that is until he saw the drawing-room at Balmoral. And yet despite the overgilding, the sociable, the busts and bibelots under glass domes and the truly staggering pair of candelabra on the right of the picture, the arrangement of the room achieves an effect vaguely similar to that sought by some interior designers of the present day. Several Victorian fashions have returned in recent years; potted palms, covered tables and homely clutter are again popular. One must also remember that such crowded rooms looked warm and comfortable by oil lighting and captured that atmosphere of *gemütlichkeit* which the Queen valued so much. Later in the century, English interiors suffered from the compulsion to load and decorate every surface; Queen Alexandra's writing table at Marlborough House had upwards of ninety objects on it. Contemporary photographs and the rooms at Osborne which remain as the Queen left them, show that despite the accumulation of bric-a-brac, she liked her surroundings to be gay and personal. The bedrooms at Osborne are mostly painted in soft colours with bright chintz curtains and chaircovers, tailored in a style which, for the time, are a model of severity and restraint.

A room such as this bore witness to the breakdown of formality which disintegrated those principles which had guided the eighteenth century designers to strive for purity of line, symmetry and balance. The advent of the machine age and the vast increase of wealth among the middle classes produced a popular taste that was bourgeois rather than aristocratic in inspiration. Eighteenth century furniture had been arranged around the edge of the room, and chairs, before the invention of coil-springing, had been stiff and straight backed; now furniture marched inwards and chairs of every shape and depth were deployed at every angle to provide opportunities for conversation of a previously unsanctioned intimacy. In the early twentieth century the cooler winds of neo-Louis Seize would blow through these crammed arrangements until between the wars 'Victorian' became synonymous with hideous. Now in our own age when we have neither the skill, patience or resources to reproduce them, Victorian articles are highly prized for their solidity and convenience if not their beauty.

THE DIAMOND JUBILEE

The Jubilee of 1887 had been a grand occasion, but its successor transcended anything that Great Britain and the Empire had known. The Queen was to every man, woman, and child the symbol of an epoch to which no other word than Victorian has ever been applied. Throughout 1896 speculation was rife as to the manner in which her sixtieth anniversary, and with it one of the longest reigns in British annals, should be celebrated, until in March, 1897, a procession to St. Paul's and a Thanksgiving Service were known to have been decided upon. Mr. Chamberlain invited all the eleven Colonial Premiers, with contingents of troops, and everything was done to achieve a note of Imperial as well as Royal pageantry. Accession Day, June 20, falling on a Sunday, was marked by special services everywhere; the grand demonstration of Tuesday, the 22nd, was favoured as usual by glorious weather; and during the entire week London was the scene of unprecedented festivity and decoration. A review of the Fleet at Spithead on June 26, and of the Army at Aldershot on July 1, were other outstanding events in a period for ever memorable.

JUNE 22, 1897

To-day the eyes of the whole Empire, and of millions of men beyond its pale, will be fixed upon London, and upon the great and inspiring ceremony in which we celebrate the sixty years of the QUEEN's reign. They will be fixed upon the revered and beloved figure of the woman who for two full generations has represented, to so large a fraction of the human race, the principles of order, of civilization, and of rational progress. They will be fixed upon one who, in a period of all-embracing change, has offered during all these years an extraordinary instance of political and moral stability. It is easy, indeed, at such a moment of patriotic excitement to exaggerate the power of a modern Monarch, and some will doubtless be ready to attribute to the QUEEN a direct influence upon public and private life which, such is her good sense, she has never even wished to exercise. At the very outset, HER MAJESTY grasped the true idea of her constitutional position, and from that position she has never swerved. Her work has been neither to initiate movements nor to resist them, but to moderate them. In her relations with her Ministers she has always maintained, and never overstepped, her constitutional rights; and her extraordinary knowledge of precedents—for her memory is as remarkable as her experience is long—has always given her a great advantage in any discussion. It is known, moreover, that for the last twenty years or more HER MAJESTY has held, in international affairs, a position all her own. Closely related as she is to many foreign rulers, they have come to regard her as an authority who must be consulted in any matters of family difficulty; and it is not in family difficulties alone that an appeal is made to her ripe wisdom. Of all this the world is dimly conscious; but what gives its special point to to-day's ceremony is the purely personal rela-

tion, a relation of real attachment, which has so long existed between the QUEEN and her people, and which, in the minds of the masses, has now grown into a feeling of conscious pride. Everybody feels that the QUEEN is something unique, something extraordinary, something of which all the world envies us the possession; and the multitude exults in possessing it. Length of days, width of rule beyond all precedent are hers, and she is ours. What can be more natural than this "heightened national consciousness" at such a time?

It is permissible to imagine some of the thoughts which will pass through HER MAJESTY's mind to-day as she makes her second Jubilee progress through her capital. She makes that journey, escorted by the soldiers of her Empire and by the Premiers of her great Colonies, and accompanied by her children and her children's children, by the Princes of her kindred, and by the special representatives of foreign Powers, through hundreds of thousands of her subjects thronging the miles of streets where for months past all sorts of costly preparations have been made to do her honour. Since the QUEEN first made a like State progress, as she passed to her coronation in 1838, what transformations! These Colonists, who form perhaps the most applauded section of her escort, have travelled thousands of miles to be here. They have come in swift steamers, which to our grandfathers would have appeared marvels if not monstrosities, from lands scarcely known sixty years ago, in answer to messages sent by that agency which, in 1838, was just beginning to be talked about—the electric telegraph. They have come representing not a few small, scattered communities, but millions of men, brave, intelligent, wealthy, and loyal. These Indians, too, children of "the unchanging East," are changed. They are proud Princes, tracing their descent back for many centuries; and yet they have become faithful vassals of the QUEEN. They are a sign and symbol of the British Peace which now, after many a struggle and one heroic episode, prevails from Ceylon to the Himalayas. And what of the swarming people, through whose orderly and jubilant ranks the SOVEREIGN passes? In her long course, happily including the neglected South as well as the North of the river, she will see every class—the Lords and Commons, the Churches, the rich, the hard-struggling professional men and traders, the workmen, and the very poor. Among the flood of thoughts which the overwhelming sight and the tremendous welcome will force in upon her one, we imagine, will be dominant. It is the thought that, though the poor are many and though the problem of their hard fate is as pressing as ever, the vast class that comes next above them is immensely more prosperous now than it was sixty years ago. The artisans, HER MAJESTY may reflect with sincere satisfaction, are now in far greater comfort than they ever were before. They have been given a voice—in the last resort the decisive voice—in the settlement of political questions; and the bold experiment of admitting them to the franchise has been unattended with disaster. Nay, they are as loyal to the THRONE as is any class of the community, and for them the preachers of revolution, social or other, have no charms.

above In 1897 *The Times* was in no doubt that the Queen was the very essence of a constitutional monarch; to modern minds some of her initiatives may seem little short of autocratic. Certainly she would have held that her prerogatives went further than merely 'to be consulted, to encourage and to warn'. She is known to have dismissed one analysis of royal power derived solely from the will of the people as 'too Republican'. Though the sovereign today has undeniably less latitude for intervention than then, it is as true today as it was in the nineteenth century that the breadth of this latitude depends very much on the personality of the Sovereign. An experienced King or Queen can still lend a seasoned wisdom to the deliberations of a Prime Minister as Sir Harold Wilson and others have recently testified.

Before 1914 when the British monarch was inevitably related to Kings and Emperors whose power was not curtailed by any democratic process, both Queen Victoria and King Edward VII had ample scope for constructive contribution in the field of foreign affairs. When the Queen met the Tsar in 1896, they owned just over half the world between them.

opposite Queen Victoria's official Diamond Jubilee photograph by W. and D. Downey. She is wearing her wedding veil and lace. The Imperial Crown was the nearest she got to the magnificence requested by her ministers and family.

The Empress Frederick of Germany (*seated*) was Queen Victoria's eldest daughter who in 1858 married the Crown Prince of Germany. He succeeded as Emperor in 1888 and died within the year. The Empress was Kaiser Wilhelm II's mother.

Like her father she was serious, conscientous and industrious and like her mother, emotional and obstinate. She was by far the most intelligent and talented of the Queen's daughters and could converse with knowledge on art, music, religion, politics, science and medicine; she read *Das Kapital* in 1879 and sent a representative to interview the author and report back. Regrettably she also possessed grave defects. She was tactless and uncompromising and, almost from the moment she arrived in Berlin, scattered criticisms of all things German without thought as to the feelings of her listeners. Germany was a growing military and industrial power and such unfavourable comparisons as the Empress frequently indulged in aroused furious resentment. She lacked altogether the gift for appreciating the other person's point of view.

Another irritant to the anglophobes in Berlin was the incessant flow of letters between the Empress and her mother through which Victoria attempted to infuse English ideas of government and democracy; it provided ammunition to Wilhelm's grandparents and Bismarck in their campaign to alienate Wilhelm from his mother and depict England as Germany's enemy. Wilhelm worshipped the ideal of the English gentleman but this collided with his fierce desire to be a Prussian autocrat and a worthy descendant of Frederick the Great. The Empress was very close to her brother King Edward VII and after her death in 1901 of cancer bravely borne, Wilhelm's feelings of inferiority and love-hate were transferred to his sorely tried uncle, whose affability and easy-going popularity he so much envied.

THE DIAMOND JUBILEE OF 1897

The Diamond Jubilee of 1897 stands as probably the most glittering national celebration of modern British times. It was a justifiable brilliance, unlike the hysterics of Mafeking night, and unsullied by the sense of appalling loss that hung over the celebrations of Armistice Day in 1918 and VE Day in 1945. It marked a solid national pride in 60 years of peace and progress in every field of human activity; 60 years in which a small island had reached a pinnacle of riches and territorial dominion to an extent unseen since the Roman Empire. It was founded on trade financed by a massive amount of accumulated capital and protected by a navy larger than the next two largest navies put together. The nineteenth century closed on an England as filled with confidence as the England of today is filled with uncertainty.

Yet even at the height of all this rejoicing there were those who held back from the self-congratulation and high-toned pride; the Liberal strain which had opposed Imperialism earlier in the century was not quite dead. Writing in 1925, Sir Edward Grey tells of a story going the rounds in 1904; it concerned a Japanese visitor to England after Japan's defeat of Russia who found his country the object of a novel admiration: 'Yes' he said, 'we used to be a nation of artists, our art was really very good, you called us barbarians then. Now our art is not so good but we have learnt how to kill, and you say we are civilised'. Sir Edward admitted to feeling uncomfortable at the time and pondered: 'Was there something very wrong about our civilisations and the virtues of which we felt so sure?' and then observed 'The Great War has given a terrible answer'.

In 1897 England stood bound by no treaty or alliance – 'splendid isolation' as it was known. On the continent the dominating power bloc was the Triple Alliance of Austro-Hungary, Italy and the German Empire. Successive Conservative and Liberal governments pursued a similar foreign policy during the period 1886–1902: since France and Russia posed the most obvious threat to world wide British interests, and German support was necessary for the maintenance of a firm administration in Egypt, it was judged advisable for Britain to side with the Alliance on most international issues. Reinforcing this inclination was an instinct that the countries forming the Alliance were stabler and militarily stronger, and that therefore good relations with this bloc was the best guarantee for peace in Europe.

In the years between the Jubilees, British imperial expansion had been chiefly concentrated on Africa. Gambia and Bechuananland were gathered into the basket in 1888, Rhodesia in 1889, Uganda in 1890 and Zanzibar and Nyasaland in 1891. Elsewhere in the world the colonial powers pushed and laid their claims at an astonishing rate. In one generation, one fifth of the land area of the earth and one tenth of its inhabitants passed into the control of the European nations. They owned nine tenths of Africa, a continent four times the size of their own, and of all of them England had the choicest cuts. This rivalry proved a constantly bubbling hotpot of jealousy and suspicion. England bickered with France over Siam, Madagascar, Newfoundland, the New Hebrides and French exploratory activity in the Nile Valley. She sparred with Germany who, conscious of her leverage over Cairo, made alarmingly abrupt demands for British acquiescence in railway concessions in Turkey and in territory on the Congo border, which England had earmarked for part of the eventual Cape-Cairo route. The most heated and unexpected of these colonial squabbles was with a newcomer to the world scene, America.

In the last years of the nineteenth century, two political heavyweights were swiftly moving up to join the European leaders. The rise to world power of America and Russia, which was to mark the new world from the old more clearly than any other factor in modern history, was by 1897 largely an accomplished fact. Some years before, statistics for American industrial production had warned British economists of narrowed supremacy and imminent relegation to second place. Seeley had foreseen this as far back as 1883 and had hoped that by welding the British Empire into a solid 'Greater Britain', England would be able to maintain her place as a power of the first class. America, hitherto absorbed in the opening-up of its own hinterland, had by the time of the Diamond Jubilee begun to search for naval bases and spheres of influence in the Pacific. Russia's great advance across central Asia between 1858 and 1876 had not been primarily inspired by economic motives but nevertheless by 1897 she had acquired the most unified empire on earth. Her industrial capability, though well behind that of America, was advancing at an impressive rate.

In 1895 one month after Lord Salisbury had again become Prime Minister, England became embroiled in a bizarre dispute with the United States over the frontier between British Guiana and Venezuela. The Venezuelans had invoked American arbitration on the grounds that England had violated the Monroe doctrine, enunciated half a century earlier by the American President of that name, to the effect that America would tolerate no fresh European settlements on the soil of the Americas. Accordingly the American Secretary of State, Olney, informed England that disregard of the doctrine would 'be deemed an act of unfriendliness toward the United States'. Lord Salisbury brushed this aside with uncharacteristic brusqueness; he ignored the note for four months and when he finally got round to replying, stated that 'the disputed frontier has nothing to do with any of the questions dealt with by President Monroe', and that in no circumstances would he consider negotiating a frontier 'which belonged to the throne of England before the Republic of Venezuela came into existence'.

On both sides hackles rose and foolish things were said. Olney admitted that America's tone was purposely provocative for 'in English eyes, the United States was then so completely a negligible quantity'. At the last moment events elsewhere in the world diverted British wrath.

In 1896 a group of Englishmen led a mounted raid into the Boer-ruled Transvaal with the intention of sparking off a rebellion. It was a landmark in the degeneration of imperial ethics, for there is now little doubt that the Colonial Secretary himself, Joseph Chamberlain, was to some extent implicated though he covered his tracks successfully at the time. The Rand was rich and Rhodes had long dreamt of British rule from Cairo to the Cape. It was true that the British settlers of the Transvaal, who constituted a majority over the Boers, could claim legitimate grievances but this did not justify such a flagrantly illegal act.

With reluctance British public opinion bit its lip while the raiders were brought to trial. But when it was announced that the Kaiser had telegraphed congratulations to the Boer President on quashing the revolt 'without appealing for the help of a friendly power' England was angered and startled. (It would have been more so had it known that at about this time, the Kaiser was sanctioning plans for the construction of a navy large enough to threaten that of England.) It seemed a clear indication that such help would have been forthcoming if requested and might again be given elsewhere. Germany was a formidable military power; isolation was beginning to seem a little less splendid.

But in that blazing Jubilee summer such anxieties were as yet too insubstantial to cloud the sky. The poet Laureate, Alfred Austin, whose preposterous verses reflected the prevailing mood of haughty assurance, was observed in early June on the lawn of his country home in conversation with several great ladies. One of these asked him his concept of heaven; after some thought he replied that it would be to sit in an English garden and receive a stream of telegrams announcing a British victory by land and a British victory by sea. The stream of telegrams was to come three years later but instead of victories they announced a series of humiliating defeats at the hands of a small nation of farmers. The sense of glorious invincibility was not to be long enjoyed.

Joseph Chamberlain was the first to suggest that the sixtieth year of the Queen's accession should celebrate the Imperial family under the British Crown and the Queen keenly endorsed the plan; in consequence none of the Kings who had attended the Golden Jubilee were invited though their countries sent representatives. On June 20th, Accession Day, she entered St. George's Chapel on the arm of an Indian servant for a simple service of thanksgiving. The next day she left Windsor for London on the royal train. On board were the chairman and directors of the Great Western Railway. At Buckingham Palace she spent the day receiving foreign envoys and presents from a host of assembled relations. All that evening and well into the night, crowds of excited sightseers, many visitors from the Continent and America, roamed through the West End of the city, goggling at the decorations.

After a hot night in which sleep was difficult due to the noise of the crowds in the parks, the Queen woke and donned a dress of black silk with 'panels of grey' embroidered with silver, with a chiffon cape and the inevitable bonnet trimmed with ostrich feathers and an aigrette in diamonds. From the Palace window she watched the first part of the procession moving off as she breakfasted. Before she left the Palace at 11.15 a.m. she pressed a button sending her personal message to every corner of the Empire: 'From my heart I thank my beloved people. May God bless them'. At the very head of the whole procession rode Field Marshal Lord Roberts, vc – 'Bobs' as he was popularly known, mounted on a grey pony and supporting a Field Marshal's baton on his right thigh. Behind him rode a detachment of Canadian Hussars and Mounties. Then in wave after wave of glittering ranks came the living evidence of the vast Empire: Giant Maoris, New Zealand Mounted Troops, The Jamaica Artillery, The Royal Nigerian Constabulary, Negroes from the West Indies, British Guiana and Sierra Leone, the Cape Mounted Rifles, New South Wales Lancers, the Trinidad Light Horse and Zaptiehs from Cyprus, the Borneo Dyak Police, 'upstanding Sikhs, tiny little Malays, Chinese with a white basin turned upside down on their heads', grinning Houssa's from the Gold Coast and perhaps best of all, the turbanned and bearded Lancers of the Indian Empire 'terrible and beautiful to behold'.

Ten minutes after the last of the Colonial contingent had passed, the advance guard of the Royal procession proper came into sight. At its head rode Captain Oswald Ames of the Life Guards at six foot eight inches the tallest man in the British Army and, according to Princess Alice, 'the stupidest'. Then in quick succession came Life Guards, Dragoon Guards, Hussars, Lancers and batteries of the Royal Horse Artillery. Even the inventive journalists were at a loss for sufficient superlatives to express their ecstasy: 'Scarlet and gold, azure and gold, purple and gold, emerald and gold, white and gold, always a changing tumult of colours that seemed to list and gleam with a light of their own, and always blinding gold. It was enough. No eye could bear more gorgeousness, no more gorgeousness could be, unless princes are to clothe themselves in rainbows and the very sun'.

The resplendant deputation of officers from the Imperial Service troops in India was followed by the carriages containing the other royals: The Empress Frederick, the Yorks, the Tecks, Albany's and Battenbergs drew resounding applause from the crowd who laughed delightedly at the grave military salutes of the royal children. After these came the state representatives riding in groups of threes. The Daily Mail correspondent Mr W. G. Stevens describes the arrival of the Royal Family at St. Pauls: 'Already the carriages were rolling up full of the Queen's children and her children's children. But we hardly looked at them. Down there, through an avenue of eager faces through a storm of whitewaving handkerchiefs, through roaring volleys of cheers, there was approaching a carriage drawn by eight cream-coloured horses. The roar surged up the street keeping pace with the eight horses. The carriage passed the barrier; it entered the churchyard; it wheeled left and then right; it drew up at the very steps of the Cathedral; cheers broke into screams and enthusiasm swelled to delirium' . . . 'and there . . . and there' – was a little, quiet flushed, old lady. 'So very quiet, so very grave, so very punctual, so unmistakably and every inch a lady and a Queen. Almost pathetic, if you will, that small black figure in the middle of these shining cavaliers, this great army, this roaring multitude; but also very glorious'. One would like to think that much as the crowd were dazzled by the panoply of their Empire, the sight of that happy old woman touched them more. The Queen, not given to misinterpreting crowd moods, noted that 'every face seemed to be filled with real joy' and they probably were.

The service took place on the steps of St. Pauls since the Queen was too lame to climb them. On the steps were the two Archbishops, the Bishop of London, the Prime Minister Lord Salisbury, Mr Balfour, Mr Chamberlain, 500 choristers, two bands, members of the government, and, massed beside and between the pillars of St. Pauls itself, thousands more. Every window and rooftop was crammed to the point of suffocation. On the left of the Cathedral an entire warehouse had been demolished and a special stand erected. It is estimated that by some means or other, nearly fifteen thousand people jammed themselves into that small area. After the Te Deum (Albert's again) the Old Hundredth was sung followed by the National Anthem. The Archbishop of Canterbury, on an impulse, called for three cheers for the Queen; they were audible from Trafalgar Square.

After the service was over, the procession of troops and carriages moved on to the Mansion House and thence over London Bridge, through the poor districts on the South Bank, and back to Buckingham Palace. In the evening there was a large dinner party at Buckingham Palace. On the Queen's table stood a nine foot high display of nearly 60,000 orchids from every part of the Empire, formed in the shape of a crown. The next day she received loyal addresses from both Houses of Parliament and civic dignitaries; in the late afternoon she travelled back to Windsor. En route, at her special request, specially erected stands were filled with 10,000 school children who, primed with milk, buns and sweets sang the National

Anthem. The Queen, despite her exhaustion, seemed to enjoy it; no doubt it made a welcome change from the weighty dullness of official addresses.

The last great event of the Diamond Jubilee celebrations was the naval review at Spithead. The Queen was not present but was represented by the Prince of Wales. In all, about 165 ships took part, riding at ease in four long lines and two short ones; they were manned by 40,000 officers and men. The combined length of ships in line was thirty miles. The most impressive aspect of this tour-de-force was that it had been achieved without taking one vessel from either the Mediterranean, the China Seas, India, Australia or North America. At night they were lit up and provided more subject material for the rhapsodic pen of the same Mr. Stevens of the Mail (who must by now have been even more exhausted than his Queen): 'Still they came on – fresh wonders of grace and light and splendour stretching away, still endlessly as in the daytime till they became a confused glimmer six miles away'. The display of all this might was watched closely by foreign eyes, and not least by those from across the North Sea.

It was in some ways a pity that the tired old Queen lived on for four years after her greatest triumph. Though in doing so she survived to see General Gordon avenged by the victory at Omdurman in 1898, she also experienced, along with her country, the jarring shock provided by the series of ignominious disasters at the start of the Boer War, the conclusion of which she would not live to see. 'Black Week', as it came to be known, was indeed the fall after so much pride. Recent British involvement in South Africa had savoured less of the old Imperialist thinking of the eighties than of money-grubbing and profit lust, and an uneasy sense arose in the back of many minds of base motives and perverted patriotism. It revealed among other things an army hopelessly ill-prepared for modern war, and an alarmingly violent worldwide hostility to the complacent island race. After Black Week, Englishmen would never again feel themselves to be the undisputed rulers of the earth.

Even by 1897, Britain's lead in industrial production had been seriously narrowed and her potential, even at full capacity, could never hope to compete with the new giants once these had successfully begun to develop. Seeley's hope for a 'Greater Britain' depended essentially on the wills of the colonies being subordinated to the desires of the mother country, a scheme increasingly rejected by the white populations of the Empire, who had lobbied for and in one case got, a degree of self government since the mid-nineteenth century. The superb contribution made by the Empire in the Great War, and after it, the admission of the white dominions to the League of Nations, strengthened the convictions of the colonies that they had a right to order their own affairs. Even without the Great War, it's expenditure in blood, money and confidence and the loss of foreign markets, the increasingly powerful concept of self-determination would have ensured the impossibility of the 'Greater Britain' that the earlier Imperialists had envisaged.

The Diamond Jubilee was for Great Britain the last confident celebration of unchallenged power. The innocence and complacent optimism, the fierce pride in national achievement and the sense of invincibility that marked that extraordinary day in 1897 seem to modern minds fascinating, poignant and perhaps a little comic, for with the wisdom of hindsight, we know how quickly all that glory was to be 'one with Nineveh and Tyre'. Yet it was not all vain boasting. They had known their moments, these Victorians, and their stupendous achievements constituted a solid edifice which, seventeen years after the Jubilee, enabled their country to survive the greatest blood-letting in history. Great Britain entered the First War as the world's leading creditor nation and emerged as it's leading debtor having exhausted the accumulated treasure of a century of peace.

It was not only a material strength; the Victorian age *did* engender a certain robustness of character, an unquestioning sense of duty founded on values that have largely disappeared today; values which are now regarded, with a peculiar ambivalence, as both magnificent and unsound. Walter Page, the American Ambassador in London, describes how in late 1914, these Victorians, some a little elderly now, called in droves at his office asking 'if I can make an enquiry in Germany for "my son" or "my grandson" – "he's among the missing". They never weep; their voices do not falter. Not a tear have I seen yet. They take it as part of the price of greatness and of empire. You guess at their grief only by their reticence. They use as few words as possible and then courteously take themselves away. It isn't an accident that these people own a fifth of the world. Utterly unwarlike, they outlast anybody else when war comes'. And in 1917, twenty years after the Diamond Jubilee when the old Queen had been in her coffin sixteen years and the country faced the most critical moment of the war, did a little of Victoria's spirit survive – that spirit which had dismissed the possibilities of defeat in an earlier, smaller war as non-existent? For when the fine sentiments of 1897 were put to the test, they were found to be rather more than idle pomp.

O King of kings.

THE JUBILEE HYMN.

APPOINTED TO BE USED IN ALL CHURCHES AND CHAPELS

ON SUNDAY, JUNE 20, 1897.

Written by the late BISHOP OF WAKEFIELD.

Set to Music by SIR ARTHUR SULLIVAN.
(Facsimile of the Original MS.)

Stately ♩ = 72

W. Walsham Wakefield.

Arthur Sullivan May 1897

O King of kings, Whose reign of old
　Hath been from everlasting,
Be'ore Whose throne their crowns of gold
　The white-rob'd saints are casting;
While all the shining courts on high
　With Angel songs are ringing,
Oh let Thy children venture nigh,
　Their lowly homage bringing.

2 For every heart, made glad by Thee,
　With thankful praise is swelling;
And every tongue, with joy set free,
　Its happy theme is telling.
Thou hast been mindful of Thine own,
　And lo! we come confessing—
'Tis Thou hast dower'd our queenly throne
　With sixty years of blessing.

3 Oh Royal heart, with wide embrace
　For all her children yearning!
Oh happy realm, such mother-grace
　With loyal love returning!
Where England's flag flies wide unfurl'd,
　All tyrant wrongs repelling;
God make the world a better world
　For man's brief earthly dwelling!

4 Lead on, O Lord, Thy people still,
　New grace and wisdom giving,
To larger love, and purer will,
　And nobler heights of living.
And, while of all Thy love below
　They chant the gracious story,
Oh teach them first Thy Christ to know,
　And magnify His glory. *Amen.*

The Portraits of Author and Composer are from Photographs by Window and Grove, London, and Kilpatrick, Belfast.

opposite The Bishop's rather banal verse replaced an earlier attempt by the Poet Laureate Alfred Austin, which Sullivan rejected as unworthy of his music. On such occasions Austin's work could achieve heights of sublime bathos.

right The cult of size; in 1897 it scarcely needed such statistics to hammer the point home.

Sixty Years Ago and Now

BY ALFRED T. STORY.

THE British Empire this month celebrates an event which it would be hard, if not impossible, to parallel in the history of Europe—that is, the sixtieth anniversary of the accession to the throne of the sovereign of one of the leading nations of the world. But when the fact is thus stated, more than half the significance of the event is lost sight of. It is a common observation, as indicating the extent of the British Empire, that the sun never sets on the dominions which own the sway of Queen Victoria; but we only begin to grasp the extent of those dominions when we have tabulated them a little. Thus the three largest empires in the world are the Russian, Chinese, and British. China is generally regarded as the most populous country in the world, and Russia as having the greatest extent of territory; but in both these particulars the British Empire bears off the palm, as will be seen by the annexed figures:—

	Sq. miles.	Population.
British Empire	8,857,421	320,000,000
Russia	8,450,681	124,000,000
China	6,003,703	300,000,000

Of course, these figures cannot be taken as perfectly exact, but they are approximately

EXTENT OF POPULATION THEN AND NOW.

below left In 1887 the Prince had attempted to harness Jubilee enthusiasm by collecting for the Imperial Institute; contributions were small and he lost interest. In Diamond Jubilee year he tried again and this time raised £228,000, in the first year, for a fund for the country's hospitals.

"IN THE QUEEN'S NAME."

THE PRINCE OF WALES'S FUND.

The following donations were received at the *Daily Graphic* office:—

Collected by Mrs. Nott, 20, Romney Street, S.W.:—From a few friends of Miss Nott 0 5 0
Mr. and Mrs. W. M. Brady... ... ... 0 10 0
Collected by Mrs. E. Smith, 142, Loughborough Road:—A. D. S., 10s. 6d.; W. S., 10s. 6d.; E. Smith, £1 1s.; L. A. Brown, 1s.; H. Woolven, 1s.; A. T., 1s.; W. Shelley, 1s.; H. Bartlett, 1s.; J. H. Braithwaite, 1s.; J. Cooper, 1s.; J. H. Watkins, 1s. 2 10 0
Collected by Mr. Ralph C. V. Palmer, Sunnyside, Charleville Circus, Sydenham:—Mr. Ralph C. V. Palmer, 2s.; Mr. Francis G. Palmer, 2s. 6d.; Mrs. C. S. Palmer, 2s. 6d.; Mr. Francis N. Palmer, 2s.; Mrs. Crisford, 3s.; Mrs. Gurney, 2s.; Miss L. Shippey, 1s. ... 0 15 0
Collected by Miss M. Tanner, 29, Pelham

HYMN FOR JUNE 20TH, 1897.

Father, on this glad day,
Look on Thy child, we pray;
Be Thou her strength and stay,
　As Thou hast been.
All through the gracious past
Thy love was round her cast—
On Thee, when blew death's blast,
　She, lone, did lean.

Grant her, through suffering wise,
Prudent, to turn her eyes,
Where, 'neath eternal skies,
　Spread pastures green.
Father of dawn and day,
Bring her upon her way;
Hear, when her people pray—
　God save our Queen.

J. J. B.

[Music to this Hymn has been written by Dr. A. H. Mann, Mus. Doc., Organist of King's College, Cambridge.]

London Theatres.

(For fuller information see opposite page.)

Adelphi.—8.15: La Dame aux Camelias.
Court.—8.30: Caste.
Covent Garden.—8: Tannhauser.
Criterion.—8.30: A Breezy Morning; 9: David Garrick.
Gaiety.—8: The Circus Girl.
Haymarket.—8.40: A Marriage of Convenience.
Her Majesty's.—8: The Red Lamp; The Balladmonger.
Lyceum.—8: Madame Sans-Gêne.
Prince of Wales's.—8.15: La Poupée.
Savoy.—7 40: Old Sarah; 8.20: The Yeomen of the Guard
St. James's.—8: The Princess and The Butterfly.
Terry's.—8.30: The French Maid.
Vaudeville.—8.15: Round a Tree; 9: A Night Out.
Garrick.—8.15: The Lady Lawyer; 9: My Friend the Prince.
Shaftesbury.—8: The Yashmak.
Strand.—8: Dr. Johnson; 9: All Alive Oh!

TO OUR READERS.

The Commemoration Festivals throughout the Country will be fully illustrated in the "Daily Graphic" from day to day.

TOPICS OF THE DAY.

THE FOREIGNER AND THE JUBILEE.

Very pleasant reading have been the foreign newspapers during the last day or two. It was, of course, to be expected from the practised courtesy of our Continental contemporaries that they would offer us gracefully-worded congratulations on our national festival and would say polite things about our Queen; but their friendly expressions have travelled far beyond these conventional limits. On all sides we meet with the clearest evidence that the Continental mind has grasped the political facts by which our jubilation has been inspired and justified. In some respects, indeed, the average foreigner has been even more impressed than the average Englishman. To us the survey of the Sixty Years' Reign and of the microcosm of Empire with which we have filled our streets has been a source of subjective complacency. It has told us nothing we did not know before; it has been prized for no ulterior purpose. To the foreigner, however, it has been a revelation. He has been enabled to realise for the first time the stability of English institutions, the immensity of the British Empire, and, finally, the strength of the bonds by which the family of nations owing allegiance to the British Crown is united. It is not difficult to understand how this picture affects him. In domestic politics he is habituated to a sort of seismic existence; in foreign politics his calculations are bounded by the system of European alliances. The isolation of England has been to him a guarantee of English impotence. He now finds that England has sources of strength in her internal social peace and in the enthusiastic loyalty of her Colonies by the side of which the alliance of a Continental Power, or even of a group of Continental Powers, is of small consequence. In a word he has realised that Splendid Isolation is not an empty British boast.

JAPAN AND HAWAII.

Japan is likely to defeat her own ends if it be true that she has addressed a bellicose remonstrance to the United States Government on the subject of the annexation of Hawaii. Public opinion in the States does not, apparently, look with enthusiasm upon the Treaty, but the feeling in favour of it would certainly be stiffened were any attempt made by a foreign Power to obstruct its ratification. The wisdom of the annexation is very doubtful. The United States will gain nothing except increased responsibilities, and no one can say what these responsibilities may lead to. The problem of governing the islands will be full of difficulty from the commencement, and as time goes on these difficulties will not diminish. Japan would act wisely if she left these considerations to sink into the American consciousness, and contented herself with reserving, politely but firmly, the rights of her nationals in the islands. An attempt to dictate to the United States can only be resented, and will strengthen the case of the annexationists by its suggestion of a possible Japanese Republic in Hawaii, leading eventually to Japanese Annexation.

THE PRINCESS'S GUESTS.

Happy as was the gracious and kindly thought of the Princess for the deserving poor in its inception, its realisation has been no less felicitous. If there is sadness in the thought that we have so many in our midst with whom meagrely satisfied hunger is the rule rather than the exception, there would have been a deeper sadness still in the reflection that this period of great national rejoicing had passed without amelioration of this hard lot. But for the timely interposition of the Princess this might very probably have happened, and the nation, as well as the hungry gainers by her bounteous foresight, are indebted to her for the removal of such a reproach. In spite of the many difficulties in the way of organising so large a scheme all seems to have passed off with as complete success as the pageant of Tuesday. It was a charming crown to the good work that her Royal Highness should grace these humble feasts with her presence, and most of all that her first visit should be to the crippled children of the East-end. Their gratitude is probably the richest, as it is the most appropriate reward the Princess would desire.

SLAVERY UNDER THE BRITISH FLAG.

It is impossible to feel satisfied with the condition of our East African possessions as disclosed by yesterday's debate. In the islands of Zanzibar and Pemba a halting attempt has indeed been made to abolish the status of slavery, but on the mainland no steps seem to have been taken to get rid of this disgrace to our flag. On the contrary, there is indisputable evidence that British officials are actually engaged in capturing runaway slaves and restoring them to their masters. Whatever the social and economic difficulties in the way of abolishing slavery may be, this scandal ought not to continue. There was a tendency on the Government bench last night to speak as if the problem of slavery in Zanzibar was entirely unique; but a problem very similar in its main features had to be faced by Englishmen in India, and was solved three-quarters of a century ago. The solution, in fact, of such problems as these is one of the principal glories of British administration all the world over, and there must be something wrong when Ministers of the Crown have to speak in the apologetic tone adopted last night by Mr. Curzon and Mr. Balfour. That Sir Arthur Hardinge is an official of exceptional ability no one for a moment denies, but he would be more than human if his theoretical approval of the institution of slavery did not affect his efforts for its practical abolition. It surely is not impossible to find for this distinguished servant of the Crown some post where his personal opinions do not run counter to his official duty.

SOUTH AFRICAN CONCORD.

President Kruger's happy thought of releasing his last two Reformers on Queen's Day is not the only sign of a return to a state of grace. In the Cape Parliamentary reports which have just reached this country we find Mr. Sauer represented as stating that "there appears to be a disposition on the part of the South African Republic to consider favourably the question of allowing South African produce to enter their territory free; on some articles the duties have already been taken off and on others the duties have been considerably reduced." It is pleasant to see that the Cape Assembly on hearing this declined to take a step which might have led to more friction. The Transvaal's duty on Cape tobacco having been resented by the Cape tobacco growers, it was proposed to adopt retaliatory tactics; but this course the Assembly wisely and temperately refused to take before approaching the Transvaal in a less aggressive fashion. President Kruger may be sure that any overtures on his part towards a more harmonious understanding between the South African communities will be heartily approved and supported in this country; and we sincerely hope no indiscreet utterances here or elsewhere may have the effect of producing more of the discord that has so greatly interfered with South African progress in the past.

MILITARY GAMEKEEPERS.

A new use has been discovered for the United States Army. A detachment of troopers has been sent to Colorado, not to crush the beetle, but to guard the buffalo. Big game hunters have warred so assiduously on the buffalo that it is in imminent danger of extinction. There are said to be only forty living specimens left, but there is a happy omen in that number, since it is suggestive of Immortals, and now that the *bos Americanus* has been taken under the protection of the Stars and Stripes, he will in all probability begin to increase and multiply. The notion of converting Government troops into gamekeepers is decidedly original, and if our recollection of the works of Fenimore Cooper and Mayne Reid serve us aright, ought to provide the soldiers of the Republic with livelier experiences than usually fall to their lot in these degenerate days.

The Lord Chamberlain requests us to state that it is impossible to reply to the innumerable letters which he has received on the subject of Her Majesty's Garden Party.

LORD DUFFERIN AND THE CABOT MEMORIAL.

Responding to the toast of his health proposed in a complimentary speech by Sir Michael Hicks Beach at the luncheon at Bristol yesterday in connection with his laying of the foundation stone of the Cabot Memorial Tower, Lord Dufferin said there was certainly no community in England better entitled than citizens of Bristol to do honour to the memory of the great maritime adventurer, as from the very ancient days they had been the pioneers of naval enterprise, and among the powerful founders of England's power u, on the high seas. It was impossible to disassociate Cabot's voyage from the earlier one of Columbus, but while in the hold of Columbus's caravel, great and good as was the man himself, there lurked the Inquisition, slavery, the carnage of Cortez and Pizarro, the devastating policy of successive Spanish viceroys, and a permanent instability of affairs, all the elements which unite in constituting a free God-fearing State and a mighty nation, in developing that prosperity and ordered government which are born of honest industry, found their way to the New World through the instrumentality of John Cabot and the honest Bristol seamen who accompanied him.

HEAVY THUNDERSTORM IN LONDON.

The heat of the last two or three days culminated in a heavy thunderstorm yesterday afternoon. In Westminster the thermometer in the shade registered 89deg. in the course of the morning, but the temperature decreased several degrees during the afternoon. At two o'clock and again at about four o'clock the clouds became very threatening, and a thunderstorm seemed to be impending. It was, however, not until about five o'clock in the afternoon that the thunderstorm was felt in Westminster. The lightning was first seen in the north-west of London, and the storm gradually travelled to the southward. At about 5.30 p.m. the central part of the storm was over Westminster, and the flashes of lightning were followed almost instantaneously by thunder. The early part of the storm was not accompanied by rain, but there was a fairly heavy downpour between 5.30 and 6 p.m., and the storm although not heavy was still continuing. The weather telegrams received by the Meteorological Office last evening showed that a cool northerly wind was blowing over the greater part of our islands, and it appeared likely to spread over the entire country. In London the air was very close throughout the evening.

THE FIGHTING IN MASHONALAND.

Sir Alfred Milner, High Commissioner at the Cape, who on Wednesday telegraphed informing Mr. Chamberlain of further fighting in Mashonaland and the casualties which resulted, yesterday supplemented his despatch by a message as follows:—"Referring to my former telegram I regret to report that Troopers Irwin and Benison died 21st June." These troopers were returned as wounded in the original despatch.

The publication of Mr. Holmes' book "Queen Victoria," has been postponed for a short time in order that a notice of the commemoration of Her Majesty's long reign may be included in the final chapter.

SENOR CANOVAS, the Spanish Premier, has recovered from his indisposition. On Wednesday he had an audience of the Queen Regent.

THE Duchess of Saxe-Coburg-Gotha, the Grand Duke and Grand Duchess of Hesse, and the Grand Duke and Grand Duchess Serge of Russia, visited the Lemercier Gallery, New Bond Street, yesterday.

GENERAL H.R.H. the Duke of Connaught, Colonel-in-Chief of the Inniskilling Dragoons, received at Buckingham Palace yesterday afternoon the following officers of the regiment:—General Sir Charles Shute, K.C.B., Lieut.-Colonel Green Thompson, Major Page-Henderson, Captain Yardley, Captain Mosley, Lieutenant Jackson, Lieutenant Holland, Lieutenant Haig, Lieutenant Morse, Lieutenant Ansell, Second-Lieutenant Harris.

BLACKWALL TUNNEL OPENED. — The Blackwall Tunnel was opened for traffic at ten o'clock yesterday morning.

DEATH OF SIR H. GOOCH.—Sir H. D. Gooch (second baronet) died yesterday afternoon at his residence, Clewer Park, Windsor, after a rather short illness. The deceased baronet was fifty-six years of age, and succeeded his father, Sir Daniel Gooch, of railway fame, in 1889. He is succeeded by his only son, Daniel Fulthorpe Gooch, who was born in 1869.

DEATH OF A PARNELLITE M.P.—A Parliamentary vacancy has been caused in the South Division of Roscommon by the death of Mr. Luke Patrick Hayden. Mr. Hayden, who was chairman of the Town Commissioners of Roscommon, first entered Parliament in 1885, sitting for South Leitrim until 1892, when he became member for Roscommon (South). He was a strong Parnellite, and at the last election had for an opponent Mr. John Dillon, whom he defeated by 954 votes.

THE QUEEN AND THE FANMAKERS' COMPANY.—In connection with the recent Fan Exhibition the Queen has been graciously pleased to accept the prize fan which the Master, Wardens, and Court of Assistants of the Worshipful Company of Fanmakers sent through Mr. Homewood Crawford, the chairman of the exhibition committee, for Her Majesty's acceptance. The leaf of the fan was worked by Miss L. Oldroyd, of Deane Manor, Chilham, Kent, a lady member of the Company, and is composed of Maltese lace, cream silk, with gold thread and spangles, and bears eight heraldic badges, and the fanstick was beautifully carved in ivory, inlaid with gold, by Mr. Robert Gleeson (of Messrs. Duvelleroy), also a member of the Company, the fan being rivetted with diamonds, and enclosed in a handsome case with crown and Royal initials in 18-carat gold. In acknowledging the receipt of the fan Lieut.-Colonel Sir Arthur Bigge, by command of the Queen, expressed Her Majesty's thanks for the gift and her gratification that the fan was of entirely British work. Mr. Crawford was commanded to convey to Miss Oldroyd and Mr. Gleeson the Queen's congratulations upon the artistic talent displayed by them respectively.

OUR NOTE BOOK.

BY JAMES PAYN.

The rumours concerning the Procession day—and month—are very entertaining. If clubs and restaurants have not got their waiters by this time, we are told they will never get them. Even private houses are invaded, and the fealty of our men-servants endangered by the emissaries of "servant-syndicates" for June. The temptation of fifty pounds is said to be offered for the four weeks. This is almost as bad as the tempting of cooks we used to hear of in the United States—how good ones were so rare that, unmindful of the laws of hospitality, rich guests who had dined well seduced the *chefs* from their allegiance to the host. Prudent persons, therefore, kept their good cooking for home consumption, and when they gave a party employed only the kitchen-maid. At our clubs the waiters are said to demand fabulous prices for the great day, and impecunious members are said to be offering themselves for the post. As for the struggles to get good places to view the procession from friends who live on the line of march, they are too painful to be written about. They remind one of similar efforts made in Horace Walpole's time to get seats for the Coronation of George III. He had a petition sent him from "two orphans." He began to feel for his purse. It was not charity, however, as it turned out, that they wanted, but only seats for the Coronation. He compares the prices paid for a sight of the procession with those demanded in the previous reign, and speaks of the high-water mark to which extravagance had risen. What would he say now, one wonders!

At the Coronation of George II. my mother gave forty guineas for a dining-room, scaffold, and bed-chamber. An exactly parallel apartment, only with rather a worse view, was this time set at three hundred and fifty guineas—a tolerable rise in thirty-three years! The platform from St. Margaret's Round-house to the church door, which formerly let for forty pounds, went this time for two thousand four hundred pounds! Still more was given for the inside of the Abbey. The prebends would like a Coronation every year. The King paid nine thousand pounds for the hire of jewels; indeed, last time it cost my father fourteen hundred to bejewel my Lady Orford. A single shop now sold six hundred pounds sterling worth of nails—but nails are risen; so is everything, and everything adulterated. If we conquer Spain, as we have done France, I expect to be poisoned.

ANOTHER JUBILEE SUGGESTION.

SIR,—Twenty-seven years and eleven months ago I sent a joke to your paper. It did not then appear, but in January, 1882, there was a joke something like it. The joke was not a very long one, for it only occupied the space of three lines. For this article, or suggested article, I have received *no remuneration whatever!* I would not now distress your generous nature by reminding you of this; I would only suggest that the Royal Procession will pass your office, 85, Fleet Street, on June 22, and that a few seats, for my wife, my sister-in-law, my five eldest daughters, my cousin's aunt by marriage, my godfather's stepson's niece, and myself, would be a slight return for that joke, and an encouragement to me to send further contributions.

I am, Sir, your obedient servant,   OWEN DEED.

[We should, of course, have invited our intending contributor and his relatives, had he not omitted his address.—ED.]

JUBILEE BOOTS.

A Pendant to Matinée Hats.

[" An author has devised a cork golosh, 4½ inches high and weighing 10 oz. to the pair, for the use of short persons, who wish to view the procession and find themselves in the back rows."—*Daily Paper*.]

ZACCHÆUS now no more need climb
   A tree or lamp-post handy,
Nor seek an eminence sublime
   To make his *locus standi.*

A simple means has been evolved
   By genius too long latent;
The dwarf sightseer's *crux* is solved
   In this, the latest patent.

A writer sells to those who'll buy
   (The *Daily Mail* announces)
A cork golosh five inches high,
   That weighs as many ounces.

"Boots off in front," the crowd will yell
   To each obstructive giant,
Since they obscure the view as well
   As girls with hats defiant.

If all the lieges bought a pair,
   One scribe in luck would revel;
But we should all be "as you were"—
   A mob upon one level!

---

above left In 1897, before the age of television, you had to be in London if you wanted to see the fun; three million visitors turned up and several commodities were in short supply. The figure of £50 for four weeks work would have seemed like riches indeed to a club-servant in 1897; it would probably have exceeded an entire years income for even by the 1890's maids-of-all work were earning a mere £25 per annum, though board and lodging were of course thrown in. Foreign observers were continually surprised at the enormous percentage of the British working class employed in jobs that created no wealth and more often than not consisted of making life comfortable for other people; one million were employed in domestic service alone though even before the First World War wages and conditions offered by factories had improved to the extent that private employers were obliged to keep raising salaries.

opposite The Princess of Wales' thoughtfulness for the London poor is acknowledged, anxieties are aired about human rights in East Africa and President Kruger releases the last two imprisoned Jameson raiders. The Lieutenant Haig received at Court is not the future Field-Marshal.

PARISH OF — WILLESDEN.

H.R.H. The Princess of Wales'

Diamond Jubilee Feast,

THURSDAY, JUNE 24TH, 1897.

⊹ MENU. ⊹

Roast Ribs of Beef.   Boiled Round of Beef.
Roast Quarter of Lamb.   Veal and Ham Pies.

—: Pickles. :—

English Ale.   Ginger Beer.

Dates.   Oranges.

Pipes.   Tobacco.

1837 — 1897

left and below Perhaps the most touching and heartfelt gesture of the 1897 celebrations was the project initiated and executed by Alexandra, Princess of Wales to give the biggest banquet in the history of the world — to 400,000 poor people throughout London. Nobody was to be refused however dirty or criminal. As always with such schemes, people said it couldn't be done but the Princess persevered.

To her rescue came the great-hearted millionaire Sir Thomas Lipton. He sent her an envelope containing a satisfying menu with prices and a cheque for £25,000. He reckoned that she would need 700 tons of food and nearly 10,000 waiters. His feasibility study worked the trick and subscriptions poured in by every post. The Princess and her husband were able to put in an appearance at only three of the many parties.

right In 1897 the Army, though small in size, still enjoyed a reputation for solid efficiency which the Boer War, now only two years off, would shake to its foundations. Not until King Edward's reign was the Army drastically reformed – by Lord Haldane who had to appease the Radicals by reducing the Army Estimates and improve efficiency at the same time. His greatest innovation was the Territorial Army, an auxiliary reserve force which would absorb the Volunteers and the Yeomanry. It was made up of civilians trained in their spare time and would eventually contribute a further fourteen divisions and fourteen mounted brigades, all as efficiently equipped as the Regulars. Haldane felt that before long there might be a need for a British Expeditionary Force for service across the Channel. His reforms came not a moment too soon.

below In the days before the motor car, a trip to London necessitated taking lodgings, either the predecessor of the modern flat or rooms in a guest house where the landlady, who likely as not, was retired from private service and provided good food and personal attention.

PRIVATE LODGINGS.

Obliging Landlady (to Major and Mrs. Totterly Syms, who have delayed taking rooms till their arrival in Town for the Diamond Jubilee).
"YES, 'M, YOU AND THE GENTLEMAN CAN 'AVE A COUPLE OF PILLOWS AND A RUG IN THE BASEMENT-'ALL, FOR TWO GUINEAS. THE PARTY AS YOU MET ON THE STEPS 'AS TAKEN THE FOLDING CHAIRS IN THE CONSERVATORY, OR YOU MIGHT 'AVE 'AD THEM."

above The Queen planting a Jubilee tree in the grounds at Buckingham Palace. One trusts that despite the somewhat anxious appearance of the eight members of her household lending moral and physical support, the tree prospered.

below The state drawing-room at Buckingham Palace. Although set for a wedding luncheon, this photograph gives some idea of how the room looked on the day of the Jubilee luncheon.

above The Indian contingent which, with their British officers in charge were housed at the Star and Garter Hotel at Richmond.

below In 1897 the Court was a distinct caste and appeared as such in London directories; in 1897 the famous Devonshire House Fancy Dress Ball took place.

SOCIETY FIXTURES.

SATURDAY, JUNE 19TH.

Military Tattoo at Windsor.

Garden Party at the Royal Holloway College, Egham, at which their Royal Highnesses Prince and Princess Christian will be present.

Lady Ellis's Garden Party at Buccleuch House, Richmond.

The Countess of Jersey's second Garden Party at Osterley Park.

Jubilee Commemoration Dinner of the Savage Club.

SUNDAY, JUNE 20TH.

Accession Day. Completion of the Sixtieth Year of the Queen's Reign.

General Thanksgiving throughout the Kingdom in Commemoration of the 60th year of the Queen's Reign.

The Judges attend the Service at St. Paul's Cathedral.

Hospital Sunday.

The Lord Chancellor and the House of Lords attend the Queen's Commemoration Service at Westminster Abbey, 10 a.m.

The Speaker and the House of Commons attend the Queen's Commemoration Service at St. Margaret's Church, Westminster. The sermon will be preached by Dean Farrar.

Special Service by command of the Queen at St. George's Chapel, Windsor. Mdme. Albani will sing Mendelssohn's "Hymn of Praise."

MONDAY, JUNE 21ST.

The Queen arrives in London.

The House of Commons adjourns for the Jubilee Celebration.

The Countess of Jersey's Garden Party at Osterley's Park

Viscount and Viscountess Knutsford open the Hampstead Jubilee Fête.

Torchlight Military Tattoo in the grounds of Buckingham Palace.

TUESDAY, JUNE 22ND.

National Celebration of the Diamond Jubilee of the Queen's Reign.

Royal Societies Club—Reception and Déjeuner in Celebration of Her Majesty's Jubilee.

WEDNESDAY, JUNE 23RD.

The Queen receives the Mayors and Provosts of the Provinces at Buckingham Palace.

The Queen receives Addresses from both Houses of Parliament.

Gala performance at Covent Garden.

The Staff College Annual Dinner, the Commander-in-Chief presiding, Whitehall Rooms, Hotel Metropole.

Royal Agricultural Society's Show opens at Manchester ; closes June 29th.

THURSDAY, JUNE 24TH.

State Ball at Buckingham Palace.

The Princess of Wales's Dinner to Outcast Poor.

The House of Commons reassembles.

Sandown Park Meeting.

The Court Circular

And Court News.

| COURT CIRCULAR.—VOL. LXXVI.—No 2168. } ESTABLISHED 1856. | SATURDAY, JUNE 19, 1897. | Registered at the General Post Office as a Newspaper. { PRICE 1s. BY POST 12½D ANN. SUB. 26s. |
COURT NEWS.—VOL. LXXX.—No. 1968.

JUBILEE DAY ORDER OF ROYAL PROCESSION.

Captain O. Ames, 2nd Life Guards.
Four Troopers, 2nd Life Guards.
Naval Gun Detachment.
A Staff Officer.
Advance Guard, 2nd Life Guards.
Mounted Band, Royal Artillery.
"D" Battery, Royal Horse Artillery.
BANDS.—1st Life Guards, 1st Dragoon Guards, 2nd Dragoon Guards.
SQUADRONS.—1st Life Guards, 1st Dragoon Guards, 2nd Dragoon Guards.
"E" Battery, Royal Horse Artillery.
BANDS.—3rd Dragoon Guards, 6th Dragoon Guards, 7th Dragoon Guards.
SQUADRONS.—3rd Dragoon Guards, 6th Dragoon Guards, 7th Dragoon Guards.
"G" Battery, Royal Horse Artillery.
BANDS.—1st Dragoons, 2nd Dragoons, 6th Dragoons.
SQUADRONS.—1st Dragoons, 2nd Dragoons, 6th Dragoons.
"J" Battery, Royal Horse Artillery.
BANDS.—3rd Hussars, 8th Hussars.
SQUADRONS.—3rd Hussars, 8th Hussars.
"O" Battery, Royal Horse Artillery.
BANDS.—10th Hussars, 15th Hussars.
SQUADRONS.—10th Hussars, 15th Hussars.
BANDS.—12th Lancers, 17th Lancers.
SQUADRONS.—12th Lancers, 17th Lancers.
"T" Battery, Royal Horse Artillery.
Aides-de-Camp to the Commander-in-Chief.
Aides-de-Camp to the Queen.
Lord-Lieutenant of London.
Headquarter Staff.
Field-Marshals.
Sheriffs on Horseback (from Temple Bar to Mansion House).
Three Officers of the Auxiliary Forces in attendance on H.R.H. the Prince of Wales.
One Hundred Equerries, Gentlemen-in-Waiting, and Military Attachés.
Deputation from the 1st Prussian Dragoon Guards ("Queen of Great Britain and Ireland's Own").
Deputation of Officers of Indian Imperial Service Troops.
Eleven Dress Landaus and Pairs.

Five Road Landaus and Fours | Two Senior Queen's Equerries by the Carriage of the Empress Frederic.

The Lord Mayor (from Temple Bar to Mansion House).
Colonial Escort.
First Part of the SOVEREIGN's Escort (furnished by the 2nd Life Guards, the regiment of the Household Brigade supplying the Queen's Guard on the 22nd inst.)
Equerry.
Thirty-six English and Foreign Princes.
Indian Escort.
The Commander-in-Chief.
HER MAJESTY'S CARRIAGE.

H.R.H. the Duke of CAMBRIDGE. | The Prince of WALES.
The Duke of CONNAUGHT.
G.O.C. Troops

Captain of Escort. | Standard | Field Officer of Escort, Chief of the Staff.
Master of the Buckhounds. | Gold Stick of Scotland. | Gold Stick in Waiting. | Master of the Horse.
Equerry. | Equerry. | Crown Equerry.
Field Officer in Brigade Waiting. | Equerry to H.R.H. the Prince of Wales. | Silver Stick in Waiting
Equery to H.R.H. the Duke of CAMBRIDGE. | Equerry. | Equerry.
Royal Groom. | Royal Groom. | Royal Groom.
Royal Groom. | Royal Groom. | Royal Groom.
Rear Part of the SOVEREIGN's Escort, 2nd Life Guards.
Royal Irish Constabulary.
Squadron Royal Horse Guards.

left The order of the Royal Procession.

opposite Captain Oswald Ames of the 2nd Lifeguards who led it. 'Ossie' Ames at six foot eight inches, was the tallest man in the British Army. The aged Lord Howe, who held the Office of Gold Stick, fainted during the course of the procession but re-mounted to cheers from the crowd.

left Official programme of the Jubilee procession.

below The Queen driving to St. Paul's Cathedral for the Thanksgiving service June 22nd, 1897. The Queen reached the City boundary at Temple Bar at about midday. In accordance with custom, her carriage halted and the Lord Mayor of London, Sir George Faudel-Phillips presented the City's Sword of State to the Queen; she touched it and then ordered the Lord Mayor to lead the way into the City. Off the picture, the Lord Mayor is in the act of remounting his horse watched anxiously by Princess Christian, who with the Princess of Wales, sat in the Queen's carriage. Princess Christian was the Queen's third daughter; in 1866 she married a kindly, uninteresting and quite penniless Prince of Schleswig-Holstein whose easy-going disposition permitted her to remain near her ever-demanding mother. She died in 1923.

Between the two Scottish servants on the back of the Queen's landau can be glimpsed the whiskered face of the Duke of Cambridge. Born in the same year as the Queen, who was his first cousin, he was once a candidate for her hand in marriage but she never cared for him sufficiently. Immensely rich, choleric, and autocratic he occupied the post of Commander-in-Chief of the British Army from 1856 to 1895 despite never having seen active service.

St James St., was by common consent the most impressively decorated street in the capital. There were two massive Corinthian columns at either end, their bases surrounded by potted palms and flower boxes. Forty Venetian masts capped with the Imperial crown stood on either side of the street and from mast to mast were festooned evergreens (no paper streamers here). Cunningly concealed within all this foliage were electric glowlamps, which the Princess of Wales was to have set off by touching a button in Marlborough House. Unfortunately on the trial run, part of the decorations caught fire and the eventual illumination was cancelled.

The Royal procession passing through
Trafalgar Square. The photograph was
taken from the roof of St. Martin-in-
the-Fields and clearly shows the
London skyline before the coming of
the high-rise building. On the west
side stands the Unionist Club which
was to be fashioned into Canada
House in 1925. The National Gallery
to the right of the picture was erected in the 1840s using the portico and
columns from the Prince Regent's old
palace at Carlton House which lay at
the foot of Regent Street and which
was demolished when he tired of it.
On the east side of the Square lay
Morley's Hotel which was bought by
the Government of South Africa in
1931 and demolished, to be replaced by
South Africa House.

The Royal Procession passing St. Mary-le-Strand, In 1897 you could
have spent a jolly evening in the Strand watching Lottie Collins sing
'Ta-Ra-Ra-Boom-De-Ay' in the Tivoli Music Hall and repaired to
Romano's afterwards for supper.

OUR NOTE BOOK.

BY JAMES PAYN.

It is curious to notice how the Jubilee procession is ousting other subjects of conversation, even among persons one would have expected to be little interested in such matters. As for people in general, it has become a rival to the weather itself, with which, indeed, it is closely connected, for if the day is wet all is over with it: the putting up of an umbrella would be the signal for disaster. All good people, however, are praying for "Queen's weather." If the rain would injure the spectacle, how much more would it damp the illuminations! I confess I am looking forward to *them*, or, rather, to the thousands that will insist on witnessing them and ought not to do so—the women and children and weaklings—with great trepidation. When one remembers the Moscow holocaust, under circumstances much less dangerous, one may well tremble and exclaim, "Would it were supper-time, and all were well!" At the Champ de Mars, in Paris, in 1837, the crush to see the illuminations was so great that twenty-three persons lost their lives in it: all of them died from the pressure standing up, and "were borne about after death," we are told, "hither and thither by the crowd."

Unfortunately the persons who have least knowledge of the danger of such gatherings are the most anxious to risk it. The London "rough" delights in them, and is a potent factor for mischief. "What is the good of being in a crowd," asks someone in one of Poole's plays, "if one mayn't push?" On the occasion of the illuminations for Lord Howe's "Glorious First of June" victory, huge mobs paraded the streets in the small hours, breaking the windows of those who had shown their patriotism by lighting up, but had afterwards retired to rest. These scenes continued night after night, till the Lord Mayor had to express a hope that the public "will be satisfied with their exhibition of general joy, since a public display of it will tend to disturb the peace of the Metropolis." The horrors of the cry "Light up!" made one poor but loyal citizen watch his little rushlights till a late hour. When he did venture to put them out (says the *Times* of that date) he prudently posted up on his door the following notice: "Two o'clock—gone to bed. If I am to light up again be so obliging as to ring the bell." Mr. Wilkes's windows suffered considerably, but he refused to prosecute the rioters, observing good-naturedly, "They are only some of my pupils now set up for themselves." He was certainly a pleasant scoundrel.

above right The Queen's procession winds down Fleet Street to St. Paul's.

above In 1896 at the coronation of the Russian Emperor, a mass stampede had occurred and twelve hundred people were trampled to death. Memories of this disaster were still fresh in people's minds.

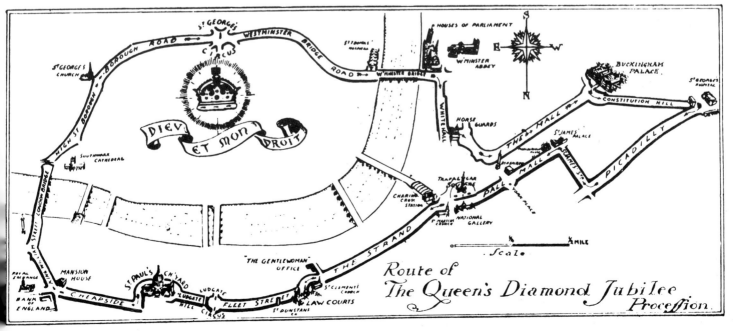

Route of *The Queen's Diamond Jubilee Procession*

The carriage of the Prime Minister of Australia starting to cross London Bridge followed by Australian troops. The building on the extreme left is Fishmongers' Hall, built when the Bridge was new in the 1830s.

opposite The Penny Illustrated Paper on Jubilee Day.

The Queen's carriage on London Bridge. Built by Rennie in 1831 it rapidly proved too narrow and in 1905 was widened by ten feet. Granite pillars replaced the old stone sides. In the 1960s the bridge was dismantled stone by stone; each stone was numbered and the entire bridge was then shipped to Arizona where it was reassembled as a tourist attraction. To the left of the picture is the Adelaide Buildings, old home of the Pearl Assurance Company which moved to High Holborn in 1913; it appears to have two steeples but neither belong; the one resembling a lighthouse is, of course, the Monument. The other is the Wren steeple of St. Magnus the Martyr, now totally obscured by the modern Adelaide House.

Billingsgate Fish Market, with its covered arches, was originally built in 1854 in a style tactlessly similar to Osborne House. By 1897 it had lost its campanile and the facade had been given a more uniform height.

above Photographs of the Queen smiling are rare and doubtless this
has helped to increase her reputation as a gloomy killjoy; certainly
when silent or preoccupied, she could exude a grim melancholy as
thick as a Scotch mist. But when in good spirits, she could tell
stories in her girlish voice that were genuinely funny. Numerous
witnesses testify to her delightful laugh. She also had a gift for tart
repartee of a particularly crushing and repellent finality, which she
reserved for the presumptuous or the ponderous; the effect of some
of these ripostes must have been richly comic provided you were
not the butt.

The majority of Victorians did not smile before the camera. The
idea of automatically creasing one's features into an expression of
causeless mirth would have seemed to them vulgar. Photography
was an instant and convenient substitute for portrait painting and
the studio photograph perpetuated the tradition of pillared or sylvan
backcloths, with the subject examining a book or gazing into space
in demure contemplation.

Although there had been celebrations to mark the fiftieth year of King George III's reign, the national celebration of a jubilee was a novelty; the Press hopefully offered a medieval precedent of sorts.

Her Majesty's infinitely touching and womanly Message to her beloved people has, if possible, increased the enthusiasm of the nation; and on every side further expressions of loyalty and devotion have been heard. Indeed, the Queen has reached the highest limit of love and popularity.

above On Procession Day, Buckingham Palace had been linked to the Central Telegraph Office and thus to all parts of the Empire for instant transmission of her message: 'From the bottom of my heart I thank my beloved people. May God bless them. V.R. and I.'

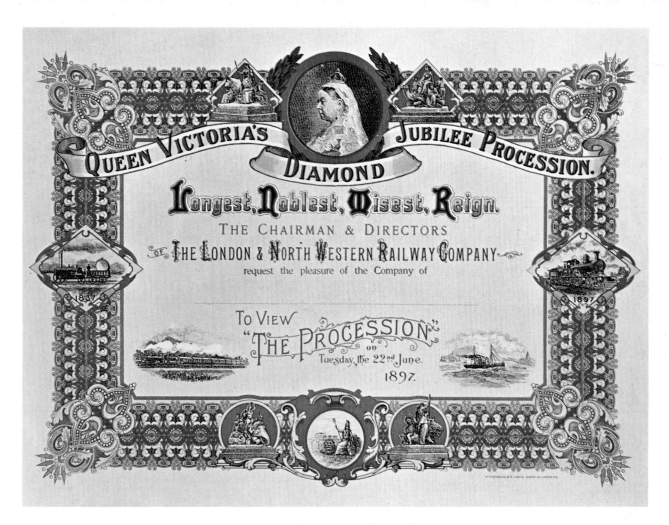

The Directors of the London Railway Company commemorate the longest reign.

Invitation to the Diamond Jubilee Ball at the Guildhall, recording incidents in the Queen's reign.

The Spithead Review 1897.

Queen Victoria's family.

RECESSIONAL

God of our fathers, known of old,
   Lord of our far-flung battle-line,
Beneath whose awful Hand we hold
   Dominion over palm and pine—
Lord God of Hosts, be with us yet,
Lest we forget—lest we forget!

The tumult and the shouting dies;
   The Captains and the Kings depart:
Still stands thine ancient sacrifice,
   An humble and a contrite heart.
Lord God of Hosts, be with us yet,
Lest we forget—lest we forget!

Far-called, our navies melt away;
   On dune and headland sinks the fire:
Lo, all our pomp of yesterday
   Is one with Nineveh and Tyre!
Judge of the Nations, spare us yet,
Lest we forget—lest we forget!

If, drunk with sight of power, we loose
   Wild tongues that have not Thee in awe,
Such boastings as the Gentiles use,
   Or lesser breeds without the Law—
Lord God of Hosts, be with us yet,
Lest we forget—lest we forget!

For heathen heart that puts her trust
   In reeking tube and iron shard,
All valiant dust that builds on dust,
   And guarding, calls not Thee to guard,
For frantic boast and foolish word—
They Mercy on Thy People, Lord!

RUDYARD KIPLING

Kipling's 'Recessional' was published in *The Times* on the morning of the Diamond Jubilee; its impact was enormous, Sir Edward Clarke, the distinguished barrister, called it 'the greatest poem by any living man'.

The Jubilee in the East – an allegory.

The Diamond Jubilee—Monarchy or Republic?

1897 was the year of Queen Victoria's Diamond Jubilee. In the *Labour Leader* for June 19th Hardie wrote the following characteristic article on the Jubilee celebrations:—

"Tuesday next will witness a display on which the future historian will dwell with much interest. From the uttermost ends of the earth statesmen and soldiers will ride in princely procession in the train of Queen Victoria, the titular head of the British Empire. East, west, north and south will be lost to view for the moment—absorbed in the world-embracing Empire. The representatives of the mysterious East—the product of long ages of civilisation and religious mysticism—will join hands with the swarthy agriculturalists of the new, growing colonies of Oceana and of the children from the backwoods of the Lady of Snows. All the pomp and pageantry of war, the lavish wealth the world has learnt so well how to produce, will be on view. Lining the route of the cavalcade will be forty thousand armed men, within whose lines the representatives of the Empire, together with those coming kings and rulers who will one day, in the providence of God, be called upon to sway the sceptre of empire over lands not under the beneficent rule of Queen Victoria. Back of the soldiers will stand millions of people who will cheer and wave handkerchiefs as the royal personages pass. Symbolically, the world will be united in a common rejoicing over an event rare in the history of nations. To the visitor from Mars two things might seem incontrovertible—first, that the world was at peace; second, that the thrones of the world were firmly embedded in the hearts of a loyal and grateful people.

And yet the Martian visitor would be totally mistaken. The cheering millions would be there and cheer just as lustily if the occasion were the installation of the first President of the British Republic; the soldiers are there because they are paid for coming, and nine out of every ten of them will heartily curse the whole affair as a disagreeable and irksome additional duty; the statesmen are there because Empire means trade, and trade means profit, and profit means power over the common people. The "providence of God" which establishes and preserves kings and queens is merely that set of circumstances which happen to fit in with their personal advantage. Modern loyalty is born of one of two states of mind—fear of the common people or toadyism. There is no third explanation possible. Even under a representative system of government it is possible to paralyse a nation by maintaining the fiction that a reigning family is a necessity of good government. Now, one of two thing must be—either the British people are fit to govern themselves or they are not. If they are, an hereditary ruler who in legislation has more power than the whole nation is an insult; if they are not, they should not be entrusted with votes. Despotism and monarchy are compatible; democracy and monarchy are an unthinkable connection.

Under whose banner, then, are we serving? Acts of Parliament open with this preamble: *Be it enacted by the Queen's most gracious Majesty by and with the consent of the Lords and Commons in Parliament assembled.* Now, what is that statement—fact or fiction? If it be true that the acts are passed by the Queen, the statement effectually disposes of our claim to be a self-governing people; if it is not true, it should not be there. No man can serve two masters, and if we are for the Queen we are not for her subjects. The throne represents the power of caste — class rule. Round the throne gather the unwholesome parasites who, incapable of living an independent existence, and not having the faculty which enables a healthy human being to find support in the affections of neighbour and friend, cling to the system which lends itself to their disordered condition. The toady who crawls through the mire of self-abasement to enable him to bask in the smile of royalty is as much the victim of a diseased organism, and as great a danger to the community, as is the lunatic who has to be put under restraint in the interests of public safety. No healthy, well-developed people could for one moment tolerate an institution which belongs to the childhood of the race, and which in these latter days is the centre, if not the source, of the corrupting influences which constitute Society.

I am, therefore, no believer in royalty which has ceased to be royal. The great mind, the strong heart, the detestation of wrong, the love of truth whether in cot or palace will always command my respect. But to worship an empty form, to make pretence to believe a gilded mediocrity indispensable to the wellbeing of the nation—where is the man who will so far forget what is due to his manhood? And yet I have no illusions in this matter. We might get quit of the royal family without getting rid of a single one of our burdens. Title is not indispensable to toadyism. The wealthy Republican of New York will go through exactly the same course of degradation to win admission to the sacred Four Hundred titleless millionaires who compose the inner circle of society in that city as his fellow will on this side to be admitted a member of the Prince of Wales' set. In each case it is an object of ambition to be attained at any cost to honour or manhood. In each case the object aimed at is the admission of the fact that the suitor for the honour desires to occupy the highest rung in the social ladder. It marks him off from the rest of mankind, separates him not only from the common herd, but from the successful competitors for distinction. The desire to enter the sacred precincts of the highest society circles is the full fruition of the gospel of getting on. It runs through the entire life of the nation, and is manifest in every walk of life and in every stage of growth. The child at school must needs learn, not for learning's sake as a good in itself, but to stand well with the inspector; the student at the university has his thoughts centred on his degree, and what he learns is only valuable in so far as it brings him nearer the object of his pursuit. Workmen of all grades are asked to turn out the greatest quantity of work, not because it is a man's duty to himself and his followers to do his best, but because he will thereby earn higher wages. I might go on multiplying illustrations, but these will suffice. That which should always be done for its own sake is done with the ulterior motive in view, and thus loses much of its value.

We are trained in the selfish doctrines of getting on, and getting on means rising on the ruins of our fellows. On this is based our notions of private property in land and capital, with its consequent production for profit. And it cannot be too often repeated that thrones and president chairs are used by the plunderers of labour with philosophic impartiality to bolster up the fiction of private property. In this country loyalty to Queen is used by the profit-mongers to blind the eyes of the people; in America loyalty to the flag serves the same purpose. Law and order, by which the commoners are kept quiet whilst they are being fleeced by their masters, must have a symbol, and anything will serve. Therefore, until the system of wealth production be changed it is not worth while exchanging a queen for a president.

The robbery of the poor would go on equally under the one as the other. The king fraud will disappear when the exploiting of the people draws to a close.

Every such show as the present hastens the end. Millions will go out on Tuesday next to see the Queen. What they will see will be an old lady of very commonplace aspect. That of itself will set some a-thinking. Royalty to be a success should keep off the streets. So long as the fraud can be kept a mystery, carefully shrouded from popular gaze, it may go on. The French king was safe and was treated with all deference supposed to be due to his office until the Revolutionaries came within speaking distance of him. Then the charm faded and the guillotine settled the matter. A similar experience had been gone through in this country in the case of Charles. The light of day is too much for the mummeries on which a throne rests.

The consolidation of the Empire is a good thing in itself. It is bringing nearer the reign of democracy and breaking down the barriers which keep nations apart. But this has no connection with royalty. The workers can have but one feeling in the matter—contempt for thrones and for all who bolster them up, but none the less a genuine desire to bring the nations of the earth closer together in unity—not on the basis of a royal alliance nor on a commercial union, but on that of a desire to live in concord. King and diplomat and trader are each, all unwittingly, preparing the way for this consumation so devoutly to be desired.''

THE TRIUMPH OF MONARCHY.

UNTIL yesterday the Jubilee Celebrations of 1887 held the record, not only for modern pageantry but for its spontaneous demonstration of loyalty and affection : to-day we look back upon it with comparing minds, and find it insignificant beside that wonderful display that has just fired the great British Empire with enthusiasm. When the Diamond Jubilee Procession was first talked of, people smiled at the idea of its being possible to repeat the splendid spectacle seen ten years before. Now people laugh aloud with joy at the thought that not only has it been possible to draw troops and people from every corner of the Empire once again, but that the loyalty of the British nation has increased tenfold in strength, till it is stronger and fuller than it has ever been since an English King first sat upon a Throne. For yesterday's demonstration was little short of marvellous in that it showed how powerful may be a good Monarchy even in these degenerate days of what is called Democracy. The cheers that rent the air were more than hearty : they were a great deal more than the loud expression of a people's pleasure at the glorious scene that had been so carefully prepared for them. There was that indefinable something in their ring that told of things infinitely greater than this. They came from the heart—the heart of a nation that is indeed loyal to the backbone; a nation that from the beginning has held its head high in the pride of its might, and that to-day knows that it stands highest on the roll of the countries of the world. No description of yesterday's proceedings can be fulsome or gushing ; for it is in the power of no mortal man to paint in words the feelings of the heart depicted so clearly on the faces of those who made up the great crowds that filled the streets : bright, happy, joyous faces they were, all of them, if here and there the eyes glistened with tears as our Gracious Queen passed slowly along the streets. It was indeed an affecting sight ; and none was more moved by it all than Her Majesty herself, who, in the supreme moment of her glory and of her power, could not help showing her People how their cheers went to her heart, nor could herself keep back the tear that would break forth, though the face was happy, smiling ; and the noble head was held so proudly in the knowledge of a nation's love and deep respect. Men and women shouted themselves hoarse ; lips on which God's name had never been for years, save in blasphemy, prayed for a blessing on the Good Queen's head ; and the youngest of all the millions was taught a lesson that will be remembered long after the snowfall of time has fallen upon their heads—of goodness, and purity, and nobility of life and its reward. For in Her Majesty, as she sat in her magnificent carriage, amid all the splendour of her Court, the glistening of gold, the shining of sabres, and the pomp of Cavalry, in her quiet simple dress all of us recognised a grand example of humility, of patience, of long suffering—in a word, of Womanliness. The thought that must have occurred to all as they saw this Great Lady was of how possible it is even for the greatest to be good and pure : even for a Queen to be a good wife and mother. Many lessons were taught yesterday : none greater than that greater religious lesson embodied in the life and personality of Queen Victoria.

In so far as politics are concerned, much was done yesterday—perhaps more than most people will admit at the present time. Every cheer that greeted the Colonial Premiers and the Colonial troops ; every hat or handkerchief waved bound the Colonies to their Mother Country with yet another and a stronger band. "Hoops of steel," they truly are that were forged yesterday, and future history will tell the tale of how much was accomplished. The story of how the Colonial representatives were received has already been flashed to the far corners of the earth. In Canada, in Australia, in New Zealand, in the smallest of Colonial dependencies the humblest man and woman will feel that the cheers were meant for them. They will recognise that we would claim them as brothers in more than mere relationship, that we are bound to one another by the very closest of ties—banded together to uphold the glory and the dignity of an Empire which is verily the greatest the world has ever known. Instead of wanting to set up little Kingdoms or Republics of their own, the people of the Colonies will be proud to range themselves under the Queen's banner ; to feel that they have a right to share in England's glory ; that they are indeed British of the British. These may be brave words, but we doubt if we overstate the case. We doubt if ever was Imperialism a more dominant note than it is in Colonial politics to-day. Above all, we doubt if greater good could have been done to Greater Britain than it was yesterday by that Procession through the streets, of which, though it only lasted an hour or two, the effect will be felt through all ages. Queen Victoria is Empress of India only by name ; in spirit she is Empress of every country over which the British flag waves ; and of each of the millions who knows her sway.

The greatest lesson perhaps of all those taught yesterday is that of the Monarchy—of how well it is for us that we have a great Queen to rule over us. The greatest of Presidents and Republics could have established no Empire as is ours to-day; and it must be acknowledged by all that in our Monarchy lies our strength. And ours is that best of all Monarchies—a Monarchy constitutionally tempered. Our Ruler is a Queen who has been a mother to her people : ever ready to do her people's will when that will has been good, she has restrained them from committing great follies and mistakes ; and has exercised her power with perfect discretion and infinite tact. Those who came from foreign countries over which no Royal flag waves must have been filled with envy yesterday ; and it must have given the Republican much to think. For he saw that Monarchy—even in the person of a Queen—is to-day the supreme power of Government, just as it was in the centuries long passed away.

*   *   *   *   *

Probably there will be much jumping on the Poet Laureate's poem published last Monday ; for he seems to have a host of curiously bitter critics ; but it is certainly graceful, in parts touching, dignified, and indeed almost adequate. To be quite adequate would have taxed the genius of Byron and Tennyson rolled into one. This stanza the latter might have not been ashamed to sign :

> Never be broken, long as I shall reign,
>   The solemn covenant 'twixt them and me,
> To keep the kingdom moated by the main,
>   Loyal yet free.

Nor this :

> Their thoughts shall be my thoughts, their aim my aim,
>   Their free-lent loyalty my right divine ;
> Mine will I make their triumphs, mine their fame,
>   Their sorrows mine.

*   *   *   *   *

But Mr. Alfred Austin has nothing quite up to Lord Selborne's twelve-line stanza published ten years ago : although Lord Selborne did not claim to be a Poet. Such a couplet as

> So hast thou won thy people's hearts : they see
> Wife, Mother, Friend, not Queen alone, in Thee,

should surely live.

above The growth of Empire; after the Great War, the areas in black would grow even
larger with the additions of the German possessions in Africa.

Lady Warwick's Jubilee party at Warwick Castle was an immense success. The attractions, many and varied, included performing elephants and the Blue Hungarian Band. But nothing was so popular as "the delineation of handwriting" by a lady engaged as an expert in this department of character-reading. For three hours she was surrounded by a crowd clamorous for self-knowledge. Among the many tendencies noted as belonging to the longest reign should certainly be included the increase of interest in all sorts of divination and thought-reading, in palmistry and in fortune-telling, which has marked the Victorian era. The wise woman and the astrologist who flourished in the days of the Stuarts have very close representatives and successors to-day, quite as popular at garden-parties in London as they are at fêtes such as Lady Warwick's in the provinces.

above Daisy Warwick was a seductively scatterbrained heiress with a dull, nice husband to whom she was spectacularly unfaithful. As a young girl she had been eyed by Queen Victoria as a wife for her youngest son Leopold, for the Queen was tired of penniless sons-in-law; Daisy refused the Prince.

The Ball sounds as lavish as one a few years earlier which had been attacked in the *Clarion*, a Radical journal. In high dudgeon, Daisy had bearded the editor in his office and was lectured on the foolishness of her ways. It was the start of a gradual conversion to Socialism and the eventual dispersal of most of her fortune for the cause. She died in 1938, a plump much-loved figure.

The *Gentlewoman* salutes the Queen.

A WOMAN'S TALK.

DEAR VANITY,—The main impressions that occur to me, writing directly after seeing the Great Jubilee Procession, before generalities have had time to crystallise, are how happy and young the Queen looked, how a dusting of red sand beautifies a roadway, how gallant the troops were, and how delightfully and with what dignity every one behaved. It was as if each man, woman, and child realised with completest conviction that Her Majesty was doing us a supreme honour in thus coming among us after sixty hard years reigning in our behoof; and that we must meet her and greet her and speed her on her joyous way with respect the most profound, and the loyalest love manifested by discreet and gentle courtesy.

I never saw her look better, not even when she last went in her grand glass coach, in her robes of State and her crown upon her head, to open Lord Beaconsfield's Parliament (his last, I believe). On Tuesday, as she drove down Pall Mall, she was seated erect, without even a cushion at her back, with the roses of the Highlands in her cheeks, and a smile on her lips. She looked less worn than her own daughter the Empress Frederick; who, for all she was so smiling, appeared fatigued. She must have had a bad passage in the storm from Germany.

The Queen's mantle, too, was most becoming. It was mainly, of course, like her dress, of black silk; but to trim it there was a very broad band, or flounce, of splendid cream and black lace, which looked striking and most handsome. Her bonnet was very pretty, with its soft touches of white ostrich and lace and glimmerings of diamonds, and did not unduly shadow her face. When the sun, which, as usual, poured beneficent streams of sweetness and light upon the way she went, was overstrong, she held up a small and simple pure white silk parasol, the gift of that noble Parliamentary veteran, Mr. Villiers. Everyone has noticed with pathetic pride how Queen's weather has been our Royal Lady's portion since she came to town for her own day of days. Monday morning was dull and chilly till noon; and as for Tuesday, till just before the procession started from the Palace, we had a sullen sky of lead, and every prospect of an unpicturesque, if fine, day—one that would have made the pageant a far less brilliant display than it happily was.

From the Princess Christian, who with the Princess of Wales sat opposite the Queen, I only received a general impression of happy content; but the Princess of Wales's dress was lovely, the very palest mauve, and cream lace laid on the bodice in cuirass form. Her dressmakers, Mesdames Berthé and Yeo, had told me it was uncertain what Her Royal Highness would wear; so much, of course, depended on the weather. But it was almost a foregone conclusion that she would choose a gown such as she wore, out of the alternative ones she ordered, because the delicate tint she specially affects of this so fashionable shade is her favourite colour, and has been for years. Whether his baby Royal Highness, little Prince Eddie of York, was so small that I overlooked him in his carriage I don't know, but though I had him in my mind, I did not see him. Before the procession formed he, with his brother and very small sister, drove with their nurses to Buckingham Palace, and later all appeared on the principal balcony. Perhaps his "nerves" kept him in seclusion!

Certainly the Queen set us all a lesson of nerve—as opposed to the disagreeable plurality. There was a tense suspense quite discernible amongst everyone before she arrived; when quite naturally one's feeling was for her and what all the noise might mean to her. But the first sight of her, so resolute, so beautiful and so queenly, drove away every fear. One who was there tells me that when she got back to the Palace she looked more fatigued than when she set out. But that cannot mean much, for it was her fresh alertness that was most observable as she went down Pall Mall.

The other Royalties who flashed past in dazzling numbers were all dressed in pale colours and summerlike chiffons. There were carriage loads of children, the Connaught Princesses and their brother, the Duke of Albany and his sister, pretty Princess Ena of Battenberg, who bowed so graciously and often, and her brothers. All the little boys wore full dress kilts, and the little girls were attired, after the usual manner of Royalties, in spotless but simple muslins, and large, rather mushroom shaped, hats with white ostrich and white satin trimmings.

London must have been very much impressed with the magnitude of the occasion, and the streets along the line of route were commendably clear. By this it is meant that there were no ugly mass rushes; and that those who meant to get places, even defenceless women, got them quite easily, and kept them. To be sure, there were those who took up their positions on Monday night and went to fitful sleep on the curbstones. But others who aimed at places in important centres such as the Mall, did not get there until seven, and were able to take up and keep front row positions from which they saw everything; for the route was lined with the most kindly soldiers, and the good temper of all and sundry, even to harassed underground railway officials, was beautiful to contemplate and delightful to enjoy.

It is hard to leave the subject of last Tuesday, but it is one for often recurring to which we may all be forgiven. Besides, there are so many attendant functions to chronicle. An event of last week was the Handel Festival, at the Crystal Palace, which came to a close with a gloriously stirring rendering of the National Anthem, after "Israel in Egypt" had been sung, on Friday afternoon. The chorus was vast, enormous, almost unbelievably big; but all the voices and parts were in such complete accord and such delicate sympathy with Mr. Manns's will and bâton that they were like hugely magnified single tones. The fugue passages, the descriptive ones —and "Israel in Egypt" is very descriptive—were supremely well delivered. Mr. Santley only sang once, with Mr. Andrew Black, in that great duet, "The Lord is a Man of War"; but his was the great glory and ovation of the afternoon. Mr. Edward Lloyd was, as ever, delightful. The ladies were the least satisfactory; but then it must be cruelly difficult to sing in so curious and vast a place, and through a small hurricane, too! Miss Ella Russell was wearing much turquoise-blue both in her gown and her well-tilted toque, softened with white chiffon; and in the toque tall ostrich plumes. Miss Marian Mackenzie discarded her headgear; and her gown was one of mauve brocade, patterned with sparkling black sequins in a big and handsome design. Miss Clara Samuell looked cool in grass lawn and green silk, but an unwelcome touch of pink in her toque was a less happy inspiration than the rest. The applause Mr. August Manns received was not a whit more than his desert. The ladies of the chorus looked like a field of flowers; but still better would have been the general effect if they had all worn white, with red, white, and blue sashes, not across their bodices, but girdling their waists and hanging at the left side.

The wonderfully gallant conduct of those in authority at St. Paul's on Sunday is going to be treasured up as a happy Jubilee experience by many who got in, without tickets, to the great Commemoration Service. Two girls I heard of persevered, hoping against hope, for at least a couple of hours before the sermon began, at last to be passed in to seats surpassing their wildest aspirations, whence, according to one, a most courteous Q C., perceiving them to be country cousins, pointed out the Royalties and other persons of note, and made them generally jubilant. All they complained of was the length of the Bishop's sermon, and the fact that the National Anthem was not sung. Were the Dean and Chapter afraid of loyal demonstrations?

Nobody will be displeased that Knights have been made of the organists of St. Paul's and Westminster Abbey.

At the Botanical Gardens the fête on behalf of the Victoria Hospital for Children promises very well. On Monday it was delicious to sit under the trees and drink tea or eat ices to the sound of the band, and many people drifted off up there after the Jubilee on Tuesday. There are no end of attractions, and the care with which the whole scheme has been planned seems to be resulting most satisfactorily in success.

CICELY CARR.

The fashion correspondent of *Vanity Fair* was there to report to the ladies of England what the chief actors in the drama were wearing. Her speculation as to whether 'little Prince Eddie of York' was nervous is ironic; King Edward VIII disliked ceremony.

THE QUEEN'S DIAMOND JUBILEE
RECEPTION & BALL
BY THE
CORPORATION OF THE CITY OF LONDON
IN THE
GUILDHALL
on Monday, 5th July, 1897.
THE RIGHT HONBLE GEORGE F. FAUDEL-PHILLIPS, Lord Mayor. *Chairman*
JAMES THOMSON RITCHIE, ESQ. ALDN
ROBERT HARGREAVES ROGERS, ESQ. DEPY } Sheriffs
DAVID BURNETT. ESQ. *Depy Chairman*.

A. A. WOOD. ESQ.
Chairman Invitation Sub Committee

above Invitation to the Guildhall Diamond Jubilee Ball. The Guildhall, in Victorian times even more than now, was hospitable on an imperial scale. The Queen was a little old for balls in 1897 and did not put in an appearance. She doubtless remembered how she had dined in that great building sixty years before at probably the greatest banquet of her reign. Eating habits had changed in the years between and in 1837 the diners had sat down at half-past five in the afternoon. Then 570 people ate their way through thirty-nine dishes including 220 tureens of turtle, 45 dishes of shellfish, 2 barons of beef, 10 sirloins, rumps and ribs of beef, 50 boiled turkeys and oysters, 80 pheasants, 60 pigeon pies, 45 hams, 140 jellies, 200 ice-creams, 40 dishes of tarts, 100 pineapples and more besides. Small wonder that publications of the time were thick with advertisements for heartburn, apoplexy, dyspepsia and flatulence.

opposite Queen Victoria; a photograph probably taken in the mid-eighteen nineties. Loyal photographers not infrequently tampered with portraits of the Queen and brushed out the wrinkles.

The climax of the Jubilee: the Thanksgiving Service in front of St. Paul's Cathedral. Crippling rheumatism prevented the Queen ascending the steps into the Cathedral; plans were put forward to carry her up but these she turned down together with the suggestion that the statue of Queen Anne (centre) should be moved; 'They will want to remove my statues next' she commented. The troops from the procession were massed around the corner in St. Paul's churchyard and Lord Roberts directed operations in person before the arrival of the Queen's carriage at the foot of the steps. Up the steps leading into the Cathedral were two large choirs (visible in white), two bands, the two Archbishops of York and Canterbury and senior members of the Government. On the right of the Cathedral, an entire building had been demolished and a special stand erected in its place; on the day it was filled with Indian Maharajahs and other potentates.

The religious ceremony was short: an intonation of the Te Deum, then a benediction pronounced by the Archbishop of Canterbury, followed by the Old Hundredth and the National Anthem. On an impulse, the Archbishop called for three cheers for the Queen. Then, led by men from the Royal Irish Constabulary, the procession re-formed and moved off towards the Mansion House.

THE LOVE OF ALL THY SONS ENCOMPASS THEE
THE LOVE OF ALL THY DAUGHTERS CHERISH THEE
THE LOVE OF ALL THY PEOPLE COMFORT · THEE

1837

1897

HONOURS DIVIDED.

(*A Thought on Jubilee Day.*)

THE Force of the Empire was mustered to-day ;
    But amidst gorgeous soldiers and glorious horses,
We must not forget, *Punch* will venture to say,
    The plainest, but not the least proud, of our Forces.
"Force is no remedy?" That's as may be.
    But "the force," for *prevention*, of risk to our city,
In all this huge jostling of great Jubilee,
    Did a wonderful work to forget which were pity.
The soldiers and sailors went striding along ;
    To be drawn to injustice by glitter were snobby.
So let's make division of praise from the throng
    Between General "Bobs," and the general "Bobby."

above Punch spares a thought for the British Bobby. General 'Bobs' is, of course, General Roberts vc who was a popular figure in the Empire. He was a thoroughgoing professional who cared sincerely for his men and was loved by them in return. He lost a son in the Boer War, which he helped so much to bring to a satisfactory conclusion. He was made an Earl in 1901 and was voted £100,000 by the House of Commons. He died in France in November 1914, having gone there to welcome the arriving Indian troops; it was a strange link with the past, for Roberts, born in 1832, had fought in the Indian Mutiny.

overleaf The Spithead Review. The Fleet was the pride and protection of England; on it depended the security of the island, its trade and Empire. In 1897 its supremacy was unchallenged but within a few years a naval arms race with Germany was well under way, measured by the speed with which each country could build capital ships. It became of paramount importance to ensure that the greatest concentration of ships could be brought to bear on the area where they would evidently be needed most – the North Sea. To this end alliances were formed with Japan, France and Russia. When the war came in 1914, the Royal Navy found itself with twenty dreadnought battleships to Germany's fourteen, and nine battle cruisers against four. In the long-dreamt-of confrontation between the two navies at Jutland in 1916, the risk of a decisive British defeat was too great to try to achieve a spectacular destruction of the German Fleet; the forces on the Western Front would have been cut off, England's food supplies would have ceased and the Allied cause lost. As it turned out, the supremacy of the British Fleet was preserved and the German Fleet did not venture out again into the North Sea until 1918, when it steamed out to surrender.

left The provinces were not left out; street decorations in Bristol. Every major town and village held its own celebrations; Manchester voted a magnificent £10,000, for decorations and a breakfast party for 100,000 children. In Newcastle, £100,000 was raised to found a new infirmary and from Ben Nevis a telegram was sent to the Lord Mayor : 'Oe'r loch and glen our bonfires shine to greet with you our Queen'.

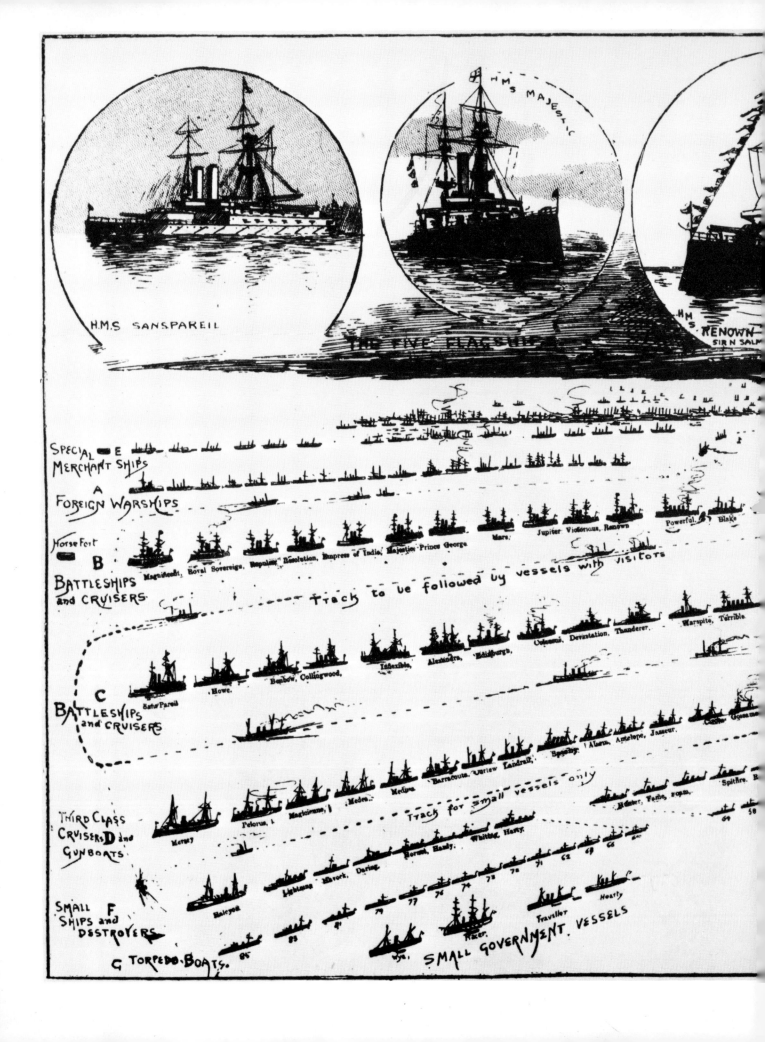

H.M.S. SANSPAREIL

H.M.S MAJESTIC

H.M.S RENOWN
SIR N SALM

THE FIVE FLAGSHI

SPECIAL E
MERCHANT SHIPS

A
FOREIGN WARSHIPS

Horse Fort

B
BATTLESHIPS
and CRUISERS

Magnificent, Royal Sovereign, Repulse, Resolution, Empress of India, Majestic Prince George   Mars.   Jupiter Victorious, Renown   Powerful, Blake

Track to be followed by vessels with visitors

C
BATTLESHIPS
and CRUISERS

SansPareil   Howe.   Benbow, Collingwood,   Inflexible, Alexandra, Edinburgh,   Colossus, Devastation, Thunderer,   Warspite, Terrible.

THIRD CLASS
CRUISERS D and
GUNBOATS

Mersey   Pelorus,   Magicienne,   Medea.   Medusa   Barracouta, Marlow Landrail,   Speedy, Alarm, Antelope, Jaseur,   Spitfire, B

Track for small vessels only   Hunter, Forte, rope.

SMALL F
SHIPS and
DESTROYERS

Halcyon   Lightning Havock, Daring.   Hornet, Handy.   Whiting, Hasty,   Traveller   Hearty

Racer.   SMALL GOVERNMENT VESSELS

G TORPEDO BOATS.

HMS ALEXANDRA

HMS MAGNIFICENT

...HIP

..., "RYDE

YACHTS and SMALL VESSELS

Arthur, Theseus   Thetis.   Flora   Naiad,   Tribune, Terpsichore, Sirius, Hermione,   Sappho, Spartan, Latona, Brilliant Charybdis
                                                          Andromache,

                                                                        Dido, Apollo, Æolus, Phaeton, Leander, Bonaventure
                            Diana,   Isis,   Juno, Doris   Venus, Minerva,
...tes, Aurora,   Edgar, Melampus, Endymion,   Northampton   Agincourt   Minotaur
                                                                         Active, Volage, Calypso ; Champion, Calliope, Curacoa,
Vessels with visitors   Starling   Nautilus Pilot   Sentinel
                                                    Conquerer,   Wanderer, Liberty,
                                          Spanker,   Gleaner, Ferret,   De Stuçgeon, Mutine,   Nautilus
                            Skipjack, Sheldrake,   Hawley, Gontost, Fawn, Snipper,
...de, Niger, Onyx, Rattlesnake, Renard, Sharpshooter,   Desperate,
...rd,] Decoy, Quail, Ferret, Rocket,]   Opossum, Sparrowhawk, Lynx, Thrasher, Virago, Surlah,
                                                         Skate,
...rch. Triton, Vivid, Firequeen, U Albacore,   YACHTS and OTHER VESSELS

...let
53

Seahorse   SMALL GOVERNMENT
            SMALL VESSELS

NAVAL REVIEW.
BIRD'S EYE VIEW OF THE FLEET AS SEEN
FROM PORTSMOUTH.

The Spithead Review seen from Ryde beach 1897. 185 ships lay in five avenues of four miles each. Down them steamed the Royal Yacht *Victoria and Albert* carrying the Prince of Wales representing the Queen. No one thought to include the Colonial Premiers in the Review; the Press howled over the mistake and the authorities laid on a special ship in which they followed the reviewing vessels.

Thursday, June 17th, 1897.

PRICE 6 D.

Vanity Fair

Diamond Jubilee Number

OUR LONDON PAGES.

ARTICLES, NEWS, NOTES & ILLUSTRATIONS

Relating to London Hotels and Hotel and Restaurant Men and Women.

THE RECORD REIGN CELEBRATIONS AND THE HOTEL AND CATERING TRADE.

CONSIDERABLE indignation is felt amongst hotel proprietors and caterers generally, with the action of a large section of the daily Press, in persistently writing for months before the Diamond Jubilee celebrations, that the prices of provisions and the rents of rooms would be enhanced enormously. This has had a most mischievous effect upon the hotel and catering trade during the Diamond Jubilee week, and most of the large hotels and restaurants have sustained serious loss. At the Hotel Cecil, says a correspondent, practically no business was done on June 22nd, and shortly after the procession passed the extra hands were dismissed. The same remarks hold true with regard to the Trocadero, St. James's Hall, the Prince's Restaurant, and numerous other well-known establishments. The refreshment contractors who catered at the stands had a most disastrous day. Alarmed by the silly statements in the daily papers, the majority of the visitors came provided with biscuits and sandwiches, with the result that the caterers had their stock left upon their hands. One contractor who made arrangements to cater for 500 people on one stand, and who provided an excellent cold lunch for 3s. 6d., failed to take £20, including wines and light refreshments.

It will be remembered that some months ago, when THE HOTEL invited hotel managers to communicate their arrangements for the Jubilee, all of the numerous managers and proprietors who responded stated that they were making no extra charges to their regular customers. In spite of this manifestation from the trade, the daily Press persisted in its inaccurate statements, with the result that what should have proved a golden harvest has resulted in loss and disaster.

The supply of waiters all through the festive week greatly exceeded the demand, thanks to the exaggerations of the daily papers. On Jubilee Day twenty unemployed waiters presented themselves at the Hotel Cecil alone, where the extra staff were only receiving 10s. for the day—an increase of 2s. 6d. upon the recognised ratio. In the Westminster Bridge Road any number of waiters were glad to obtain work for 5s. and 7s. 6d. for the day. The waiters employed by Messrs. Lyons and Co. are loud in their expressions of praise at their generous treatment by the firm ; and the Amalgamated Waiters' Society also desires to thank them for their generosity to the extra men.

MR. MARHENKE'S APPOINTMENT.

WE congratulate Mr. Marhenke on his appointment to the Colonnade Hotel, Birmingham. He has had many changes during the last few years, and has gained a large experience of men and things. In 1890 he was at the Alexandra Hotel, St. Leonards ; in 1892 he was in London ; in 1895 at the Portrabon Hotel ; in 1896 at the Sackville Hotel, Bexhill-on-Sea ; and this year was at the Trocadero Restaurant.

THE OLD BELL.

ANOTHER of the ancient hostelries, of which so few are left as landmarks of old London, is about to be abolished. The Old Bell, in Holborn, is a quaint structure much visited by tourists as a building which is typical of the times " when George the First was King." But the Old Bell was in existence, as an inn of note, long before the present building was erected. It is mentioned in more than one of the annals of Elizabeth's reign ; and in its capacious courtyard the Bard o' Avon more than once performed before an audience composed of visitors at the inn, and such strangers as would pay the trivial charge for admission. The front of the house bears the date 1730 ; but that part of the old house which extends to the rear, and is of considerable size, is declared by experts to be considerably older. It is to be regretted that the Governors of Chelsea Hospital, to whom the site belongs, have decided to sell it for building purposes : for the structure is still in good condition, the old oak of which it is largely built being as sound as the day the beams were placed in position. The rooms, too, are quaint and pleasant in their internal arrangement ; and the house itself has a good *clientèle*. Comparatively a few years ago there was a coach service between Chiltern and London, the Old Bell being the Metropolitan starting-point ; and those who travelled by the capitally horsed vehicle, passed through picturesque " bits " of Buckinghamshire, which are even yet untouched by the railway, and are consequently missed by the average tourist.

THE PRIVATE EMPLOYMENT OFFICE GRIEVANCE.

AN INTERESTING PETITION.

THE following petition is being circulated amongst hotel managers and has met with considerable success, thanks to the energy of Mr. Einmal and his friends.

SIR,—Will you allow us to call your attention to a grievance in our trade in the shape of the Private Employment Office, which is managed by people from other trades who do not understand our hotel restaurant business. They do not know the qualifications for a staff man, and if they did they would be acting against their own interests in sending the right man in the right place, as they can only exist by the continual changes in the staff of the establishments on their books. Every proprietor and manager knows how troublesome it is to have an alteration in their staff, and how everything is thrown out of gear by these continual changes. The Private Employment Agency cannot live out of establishments where the staff remains for years ; where, also, if there is a vacancy, it is filled up on the recommendation of the remaining employés. Many managers find it easy to telephone or wire to an agency for a waiter or a chef, but it does not occur to them that this is the reason they have to make so frequent changes, as the office, in their own interests, would not send a man who was likely to stay too long.

We do not wish to say anything of the exorbitant fees charged, but we wish to point out that it is upon these fees that the agencies live and thrive, to the great detriment of steady and conscientious workmen ; and a good staff member short of money does not get a chance of a good place.

May we beg of hotel managers, therefore, in the interests of themselves, their servants and the trade, to advertise their vacancies in the daily papers, and they will, even at the cost of a little extra trouble, find themselves considerably in pocket by securing the best available man for the vacant post. There are employés' societies who can send men at a moment's notice ; and we would respectfully ask them in future either to apply to these societies or to advertise.

Hoping we may have your co-operation in this matter, which seriously affects all employés in the trade,

We are, Sir,

Yours obediently,

LOUIS EINMAL ("Unitas")
GUSTAVE LOOSEN, Manager, Savage Club.
T. KISSEL, Manager, Trocadero Restaurant.
W. MARHENKE, Manager, Colonnade Hotel, Birmingham.
J. T. TATE, Proprietor, Caledonian Hotel.
C. F. BONNERVITZ, Manager, Junior Constitutional Club.
F. V. CONOLLY, Secretary Amalgamated Waiters Society.
The Administration of the Geneva Union.
International Hotel Employés' Society.
" Union Yanymed," Amalgamated Waiters' Society.

London, June 12th, 1897.

A NEW AMERICAN BAR.

A NEW American drinking bar was opened last month at St. James's Restaurant, Piccadilly. London is not without its American drinking bars, but the *Morning Advertiser* is assured that when its details and surroundings are completed, as they will be in a few days' time, the present addition to the list of these American symposia will be the most genuine and most perfect of the whole. In the first place its counter and appliances are of the best design and manufacture, and the goods served, of which there is a list of portentous length, are those which are actually in vogue across the Atlantic. There are long drinks, short drinks, cordials, and London drinks, so that for all there is a fair chance of variety in slaking thirst. The bartender is a well-known American, and has been brought over from beyond sea and installed in his place. The attendance of visitors was very good, the heat being sufficient to suggest the idea that one of these little drinks would not be unwelcome. They made a fair start among the large number of visitors, and there seems a fair prospect that the comfortable little saloon will be well patronised. It occupies the space, or nearly so, which was previously devoted to the old smoking-room, and will be under the control and management of Mr. W. J. Roberts, of St. James's Hall.

Menus.

The following menus will interest our readers; we are indebted for them to our contemporary *L'Art Culinaire*, of Paris :—

THE ROYAL LUNCHEON—Tuesday, 22nd June, 1897.
Potage.
Consommé à la Sarah Bernhardt.
Entrées Chaudes.
Côtelettes d'agneau panées et sautées.
Bœuf braisé, sauce au persil.
Kalbsbraten mit Spargel.
Entrées Froides.
Chaudfroid de poulets.
Mayonnaise de homards.
Roulades à la Renaissance.
Hure de sanglier à la Royale.
Entremets.
Asperges à la hollandaise.   Pommes de terre.
Riz au lait à la canelle.
Kalteschaale von Früchten.
Buffet.
Hot and Cold Roast Fowls, Tongue, Cold Beef, Salade.

HER MAJESTY'S DINNER—Tuesday, 22nd June, 1897.
Potages.
Bernoise à l'Impératrice.   Parmentier.
Poissons.
Whitebait.   Filets de saumon à la norvégienne.
Entrées.
Timbales à la Monte-Carlo.
Cailles à la Duxelle.
Relevés.
Poulets à la Demidoff.
Roast beef.
Rôts.
Poulardes farcies.
Entremets.
Pois sautés au beurre.   Pouding Cambacé ès.
Pain d'orange à la Cintra.
Canapés à la Princesse.
Side Table.
Hot and Cold Roast Fowls, Tongue, Cold Beef, Salade.
Servis par M. G. F. Malsch, *chef de cuisine* de S. M., et M. Delorme, *chef pâtissier*; et leurs aides et assistants. M. Malsch has been forty-one years in Her Majesty's service, and M. Delorme fifteen years.

RUSSIAN EMBASSY—Déjeuner du 27 Juin.
Consommé de Volaille.
Mousse de Truite à la Joinville.
Noisettes d'Agneau à la Béarnaise.
Côtelettes à la Villeroi pointes d'asperges.
Crème de Jambon à la Russe.
Soufflé Panaché.
Petits Gâteaux.

Dîner du 28 Juin.
Consommé à l'Estragon.
Potage Tortue.
Pain de Homard sauce Crevettes.
Turbot sauce Chablis.
Selle de Mouton à la Printanière.
Cailles à la Lucullus.
Chaudfroid glacé.
Punch à la Reine.
Petits Poussins poëlés.
Salade de Romaine.
Petits Pois à la Française.
Pêches à la Duchesse.
Timbales Glacées aux Fraises.
Petites Genoises.
Vatrouschkis au Fromage.
Servi par M. J. Augustin, *chef des cuisines* de l'Ambassade de Russie.

Asperges en branche sauce Mousseline.
Macédoine de fruits au Champagne.
Fraises à la Chantilly.
Gelées et Pâtisseries assorties.
Servi par M. Stevens, *chef des cuisines* du Duc de Devonshire.

DINNER OF SIXTY COVERS
Servi par M. Ménager, chez Son Altesse Royale le Prince de Galles.

WINES.	MENU.
	Potages.
Milk punch.	Tortue clair.
	Bisque d'Ecrevisses.
	Poissons.
Madère, 1820.	Whitebait à la Diable.
	Filets de truites à l'Andalouse.
	Entrées.
Marco Brenner.	Chartreuse de Volaille Diplomate.
	Chaudfroid d'Ortolans Demidoff.
	Relevés.
Château-Margaux	Haunche de Venaison de Sandringham.
	Selle d'Agneau à la Nivernaise.
	Sorbets au Champagne.
	Rôts.
Moët et Chandon.	Poussins rôtis au Cresson.
	Cailles sur Canapés à la Royale.
	SECOND SERVICE.
	Salade Romaine.
Sillery sec., 1846.	Asperges d'Argenteuil.
	Croûtes aux Cerises à la Montmorency.
	Petits Soufflés glacés à la Leopold.
	Gradins de Pâtisseries assorties.
Chambertin.	Cassolottes de fromage à la Victoria.
	Corbeilles de glaces variées.
	Gaufrettes.

Royal Porto, 1847—Sherry, Georges IV.
Château-Laffitte, 1864.
Fine Champagne, 1844.

20 Juin 1897.

DINNER OF 50 COVERS
Donné par le Prince de Galles aux grands Dignitaires de la Couronne et aux Ambassadeurs extraordinaires.
Dîner du 24 Juin 1897.
Potages.
Tortue Clair.
Consommé Printanier froid.
Poissons.
Whitebait naturel à la Diable.
Filets de soles à la Joinville.
Entrées.
Côtelettes de Cailles à la Clamart.
Chaudfroids de Volaille à la Renaissance.
Relevés.
Jambon Poëlé au Champagne.
Selle d'Agneau froide à l'Andalouse.
Rôts.
Canetons de Rouen sauce Rouennaise.
Ortolans sur Canapés.
Salade à la Francaise.
Entremets.
Artichauts sauce Mousseuse.
Pêches à la Montreuil.
Petits Soufflés glacés à la Princesse.
Gradins de petites Pâtisseries.
Savoureux.
Croûtes au Jambon.
Glace.
Melons glacés à la Victoria.
L'auffrite.
Servi par M. Ménager, *chef des cuisines* du Prince de Galles.

Evening of a reign. In October 1897, the Duchess of York's mother died having left no will. Forthwith the Queen made hers and left meticulous instructions for her funeral. The Boer War, the death of a son and the illness of the Empress Frederick saddened her last days. She died at Osborne in January 1901.